GOOD MORNING!

Lee Kinard

Lee Kinard

For the Youngs
Best wishes
Lee Kinard
11-8-97

DOWN HOME™ Down Home Press, P.O. Box 4126, Asheboro, N.C. 27204

To "Good Morning Show" viewers and fans who,
for decades of love and support,
kept Lee employed thereby helping him
raise his children and grandchildren.

In Memorium for Mother
Grace Winecoff Kinard
1907-1997

Good Morning!

CONTENTS

One .... A Cold Day in December 9

Two .... In the Beginning 23

Three........ Growing Up in Local TV 35

Four .... Foul Weather Friends 47

Five .... Celebrity Spotlight 57

Six .... The Only Way to Go is First Class 73

Seven .... Writers and Books 93

Eight.......... Co-hosts: A Matter of Chemistry.......... 107

Nine .... Community Service 119

Ten .... Moments of Crisis 131

Eleven .... Letters, We Get Letters 145

Twelve .... Memorable Moments...................... 165

Epilogue 173

ONE

A Cold Day in December

Lee Kinard hosting the first Good Morning Show in 1957.

In the autumn of 1957 WFMY-TV's management contemplated developing an early morning local TV news show. Program Director Gomer Lesch claims credit for the inspiration, but it was a tough sell in the front office.

"If my memory serves me correctly, when I told [our General Manager] Gaines Kelley I thought it would be a good idea to start a show like this, he said, 'Gomer, it will be a cold day in December when we start a show like that.' Sure enough it was a cold day in December when we started a show like that."

At Cape Canaveral on Monday morning December 16th, 1957, the United States was preparing to launch its first Atlas Intercontinental Ballistic Missile. In Greensboro, N.C., I was getting ready to blast off a different first, a brand new morning TV news show. Brimming with anxiety, I was probably wired as tightly as the guys at the Cape; what if my journalistic engine failed and the experiment couldn't fly?

Beginning a TV show of my own was the greatest thrill of my life. It spelled approval for previous performances in a way any creative person can appreciate, but there was a belly full of throbbing self-induced pressure to succeed. After nearly a year and a half at WFMY-TV, I was convinced this new opportunity could be a career-maker. Among the expectations fermenting in my psyche was a convincing message that intimated the "Good Morning Show" would make me rich. I was right on the money with that mental forecast. It has made me richer than I would have ever imagined and therein lies a whole series of tales.

Oh yes, I am quite sure that my expectations for myself and the "Good Morning Show" far exceeded those of management. They still do! WFMY-TV's pioneer General Manager Gaines

Kelley stood guard over the programming-production budget like a centurion under siege. His apprehension about the station's balance sheet was well supported. There were no easy commercial sales in those days. One month the station surged out of the red because the gum ball machine in the break room made a profit!

This little morning news show I was assigned to host and produce was a spartan production delegated to the station's youngest, most expendable staff announcer. In 1957 at WFMY-TV there was no crusading spiritual motivation to "serve the community." The viewers would later make that an imperative. Our objective was to make a TV news and information program the Piedmont couldn't begin the day without.

I didn't have a clear vision of how I would meet that goal and I never dreamed that I would be rewarded for using the "Good Morning Show" to save people's lives, encourage students to remain in school, cancel school on snow days, and challenge adults to improve their literacy. I would have been flabbergasted to learn that a newspaper reporter would characterize me as a folk hero. Being accoladed as a local Walter Cronkite wouldn't have impressed me. When I premiered the "Good Morning Show," America's most trusted man was five years away from his job at the CBS News anchor desk. As a matter of fact the term "anchorman" hadn't been coined.

As I describe the events of that first morning you're going to wonder how I remember all that stuff—I mean, it has been 40 years. My business is collecting information and storing it, but then there has always been an innate dynamic at work fostering my relationship with the "Good Morning Show." I've always heard a "voice" banging away in my head. When I've paid attention I've accomplished. When I've ignored the voice I've floundered. The voice provides courage and energy. In 1957 the voice said, "Do it and make it work." The voice is a flame, a red-hot, scorching enthusiastic elation. I don't have enough adjectives to describe it, so that is what this book is about, a TV program in the life of one man. With deepest humility I believe I was provided a ministry and I had to make good.

Viewers always ask, do you get nervous on TV? The stock answer is, "Only when I haven't done my homework." I wasn't nervous on premiere Monday, but I was anxious, excited and apprehensive. After all, the *Greensboro Daily News* printed a picture of me and Program Director Gomer Lesch in its Sun-

Program Director Gomer Lesch and Lee Kinard discuss the first "Good Morning Show" format.

day issue highlighting a blurb about the premiere of the "Good Morning Show." I wanted to succeed dramatically. I didn't want to embarrass myself and the company that was paying me the enormous salary of $85 a week plus time-and-a-half for overtime.

So what did I think about when the alarm jangled, and mine have always jangled, on that Monday morning December 16? Did I jump for joy about starting my own TV show? Heck no, I thought about how sleepy I was and it was only 6 a.m. Mercifully the first "Good Morning Shows" were half-hours, broadcast from 7:30 to 8 a.m. But, as I struggled to get moving on "the first day of the rest of my life" I discovered that parts of my body were numb and others wouldn't change gears. At that crucial life-defining moment I remembered that I wasn't a morning person.

Adolescent recollections of crawling out of bed at 5 a.m. to deliver *The Charlotte Observer* surged to a chill when it dawned on me that just waking up for the "Good Morning Show" might be a major problem. After almost 10 years in radio and TV I had never worked the early shift. Oh God, I thought, what have I gotten myself into?

I pulled on my socks and then I reached for the first cigarette of the day. A shower was out of the question. I couldn't stand the thought of water on my body. Still can't at that hour. Well, perhaps, a smidgen to wash the sleep out of my eyes, wet palms to slick back the stubble of a GI haircut, a couple of swigs to brush my teeth.

I dragged myself through this skimpy ritual rehearsing what I was going to say when I signed the show on. From that day to this my process of hosting doesn't involve writing a script. On or off camera I rehearse my spontaneity endlessly. Radio disc-jockeying taught me how to ad-lib, enterprise, take advantage of the moment and use my imagination to work without a net.

Breakfast was not going to happen that morning or any other working morning in the Kinard household. It didn't fit my schedule or my nervously —No!—excitedly bubbling stomach. Okay, finally, I'm dressed, sport coat, slacks, shirt and tie. It's 6:30 and I'm out the door. One hour to showtime I settle into my pride and joy, a brand new turquoise and white 1957 Bel Aire Chevrolet with a 220 power pack. Brand new off the showroom floor, where it was sticker-priced at $2,700. As I wound it up I fervently prayed the "Good Morning Show" would pay for the Chevy and some other toys. Forty years later I still pray on the way to work.

Okay, while I'm driving across town to the studio on that first morning of "Good Morning" let me stress upon your willing ears that there was no theoretical structure for what I was about to try. Beyond morning radio shows there was no local TV prototype. Plus, I had no formal radio and TV training. I had learned everything I knew about the business on the job, including janitoring, which was my first broadcast position. I was a youngster striving to handcraft a product that would hopefully entice viewers and then advertisers. I had been working in the business, mostly radio, since I was 17, but my TV experience amounted to a crisply defined 18 months.

By the way, if there is a lot of "I" in the first part of this story, don't get the idea that I was conceited. This is the way it was; I was "it," a production staff of "one." I'll tell you more about producing those early shows later, but right now let's cut to the chase and get to the WFMY-TV studios at Phillips Avenue and White Street in Greensboro.

My first duty was to gather the weather, news and sports and organize it. That meant ripping stories off newswire teletypes, stacking them in separate piles and paper-clipping them. There was no electronic newsroom and no teleprompter. With a handful of the "Good Morning Show's" first content I headed to WFMY-TV's Studio One. On the way I dropped by the control room to see if my crew had checked in. The technical staff included two engineers, a master control operator and a transmitter supervisor. Their job was to get us on the air and keep us there. A projectionist operated our 16mm film chain and 32mm slide projectors. An audio man turned my mike on when he was awake, and the director, when he showed up (that would be a problem), punched the buttons that put the pictures on TV.

In the studio one production assistant operated the camera and doubled as floor manager cueing me to talk and relaying time cues. He was my only contact with the director. This premiere found the Magnificent Seven production crew poised on the brink of local TV history. Seven guys were assigned to get a new half-hour TV show on the air, all of whom would have preferred being home in bed.

In the studio I stacked my scripts on the podium that was my first anchor desk, the focal point on a simple set that included a theatrical flat with the show's logo and spaces for weather information. Chain smoking, I printed weather data on a series of large white index cards, then thumbtacked them under their appropriate titles, high, low, humidity, barometer, wind. Big deal! In those days I thought the only people who cared about the weather other than farmers were housewives who washed and dried clothes every Monday. I could not have foreseen what a major part the "Good Morning Show" would play in the Piedmont's weather history.

Less than two minutes to airtime I lit a cigarette and mentally reviewed my opening remarks. Since this new show was my personal baby I was more nervous about how the general manager and the program director would critique it than how it would rate with the audience. The burning question was not how long the program would last, but whether I could fill the time! It was important just to get through this first show without making a fool of myself.

I took a long drag and snuffed the cigarette out on the shelf inside the podium. That morning I would finish a pack between the time my alarm went off and the first "Good Morning Show" sign-off. Don't get a headache figuring that out. It's a pack in two hours.

Forty years ago the studio was lit with huge incandescent floods that baked the talent. They seemed hotter that morning and I felt the first rush of sweat. On black and white TV I didn't wear makeup. I shaved as closely as possible and prayed I didn't cut myself or develop zits. I was a young kid with a face that hadn't grown the worse for wear.

I checked the studio clock which appeared to be taking its own time and mentally yelled, "Come on for God's sake. Let's get this show on the road!" To this day I do not like to sit in the studio wasting time waiting for the program to begin. I've got a purpose for every second of every hour; I'm on the factory floor only when it's necessary.

Head hidden in his viewfinder, the cameraman finally raised his right arm.

"Standby. Thirty seconds to airtime."

The audio man hit the turntable switch spinning the 78 rpm etching of the show's first theme. I have no idea what it was. We used a variety of openers before settling on a variation of "Good Morning, Good Morning, The best to you each morning!"

The cameraman shouted.

"Standby to open!"

Then his arm fell, index finger pointing straight into my eyes. It was time.

"Hi, folks. Welcome to 'The Good Morning Show'. Hope you had a great weekend and that you're on top of the world this Monday morning. WFMY-TV is beginning something new today that we believe you're going to enjoy and benefit from. We call this 'The Good Morning Show' because that's what we're going to make it, a pleasant informative way for you to begin your day. Now let's take a look at what's coming up later today on WFMY-TV, 'The Pied Piper of the Piedmont.'"

Behold! The first order of business was a posting of our broadcast schedule. We didn't open with weather or news. I figured most folks didn't want to be shattered out of their dreams by the wire service's "First World News in Brief." I wanted you to have a soft, gentle awakening, smell the coffee, light up, settle back and let me lay the day out for you gently and pleasantly. It was a different era, not at all like today's frenetic melanges, and I wasn't going to ruin it for my viewers with stress and strain fomented by whatever chaotic events passed for news. The news could wait!

So, what did the first "Good Morning Show" viewers see on their screens? Picturesquely, I was a "talking head" behind a podium. It was strictly "Stone Age" TV. We were in the video business but we had precious few visuals. That first audience saw a "cover shot" of the "Good Morning Show," a picture of the entire set including Lee Kinard.

In the right hand side of the screen I am standing behind a tri-colored podium. From the left side of the screen the "Good Morning Show" logo looms out from its mounting on an eight-foot-square theatrical flat. This icon is an eight-point star with a smiling face in the center. Below the logo viewers see the day's forecast and index cards displaying hand-lettered weather data. That was it! A few months later we would hang an old-fashioned analog clock on the front of my podium. It was our greatest innovation and viewers complained heartily 30 years later when we changed to a digital system.

What did the news look like?

Well, it looked like Lee Kinard just sitting there reading the scripts, radio news fresh from the United Press and Associated Press teletypes. No prosaic rewrites, just raw "rip and read" copy I prayed made sense and wasn't garbled in transmission. I was lucky if I caught the scrambles and typos in time so I could ad-lib around them. I never had the luxury of rehearsal. My experience as a small-town radio announcer taught me poise, flexibility and, as they say in the circus, how to "work without a net." When we actually had news video it was either a 16mm silent film clip or a mounted press photo.

How in the world did that show survive with so little visual appeal? Hokey is not necessarily a state of the creative mind. It is a state of time and resources. That first format was simple, imaginative and representative of 1950's morning radio. That's right, I said morning radio! In 1957, eight years after WFMY-TV, the 76th commercial TV station in the U.S. began broadcasting, anything on the screen was to a great degree still novel and, believe it or not, visually appealing. The medium was still in its pioneering, developmental stage. People watched goldfish swim in a bowl and roaches march across the studio floor.

Okay! Here's what the first format looked like:

"THE GOOD MORNING SHOW," DECEMBER 16, 1957

1. 7:30 OPENING: MUSIC AND KINARD

2. 7:31 LEE READS WFMY-TV DAILY PROGRAM SCHEDULE

3. 7:33 RECORD: VIDEO: CALEN-

DAR OF COMMUNITY EVENTS
4. 7:36 WEATHERCAST
5. 7:40 TODAY'S ALMANAC: HISTORIC REVIEW
6. 7:41 LOCAL CLUB MEETINGS CALENDAR
7. 7:44 WORLD NEWS
8. 7:50 RECORD: VIDEO: PUBLIC SERVICE BILLBOARDS
9. 7:53 STATE, LOCAL NEWS, SPORTS
10. 7:59 CLOSING

There is no evidence of news or weather urgency in this first format even though the "Good Morning Show" premiered in the first year of the space age and the beginning of the missile age. Why? Because the technology was not available to take you live to Cape Canaveral, or Archdale for that matter. The Atlas ICBM launch on December 17th would be filmed. The film would be flown from Cape Canaveral to New York, developed, edited and shown at 6:45 p.m. on "Douglas Edwards with the News." Similarly, there was no weather technology. The immediacy of today's top story and our ability to cover it create a dynamic of frenetic viewership. The '50s were an entirely different culture.

Historians have a difficult time defending this premise, but the fact is that every era must be considered on the basis of its own merits, not with prejudicial hindsight. There was less urgency in a world where AM radio was the major morning broadcast medium. The audience targeted by the "Good Morning Show" was accustomed to awakening to popular music and a pleasant personality before confronting the rigors of the day. My major competitor was not "Today's" Dave Garroway and his chimp, but WBIG Greensboro's "Poole's Paradise with Bob and Willie."

In late 1957 television had not become a major news source. Walter Cronkite wouldn't appear on the CBS Evening News for five more years. The top stories of the 1960s were in their infancy. Civil Rights legislation was hotly debated in Congress, but took a backseat to space. American lawmakers were more concerned about the U.S.S.R's successful August launch of the world's first ICBM and Sputnik in October.

When the "Good Morning Show"

premiered, the top story was the advancer from Cape Canaveral about the forthcoming Atlas ICBM launch the next day. WFMY-TV's initial "First Alert Forecast" warned of colder temperatures. The music was "Big Band" all the way. Bill Haley and the Comets and the onslaught of "rock and roll" had driven me out of radio. They would not drive my TV show even though I eventually relented, became a big Haley fan and learned how to boogie badly. The "Good Morning Show" played "oldie-goldies;" Dorsey, Goodman, Miller, Shaw, Monroe and the "Swing and Sway of Sammy Kaye."

In 1957 the "Good Morning Show's" target audience was white upper- and middle-class viewers. I was ordered to design my show to attract this demographic because as I was informed, "colored people do not have the money to buy TV sets." Within a few years the civil rights and women's liberation movements would dramatically alter that perspective.

So how did that first show go? I do not recall any major gaffs. The show was too elementary to screw up. I did have to run back to the news wires a time or two for additional copy, but regular updates were part of our game plan. The most rewarding exhilaration was working solo and having the freedom to talk personally to an audience of my own making. The bottom line is that I survived the first days, the first week, and the first year.

Little did I realize that fighting for survival would be a consistent day-in-day-out battle. I could not have imagined the challenges that changes in format, technology, personnel, creativity and social issues would trigger. I had no way of knowing how the world would change through the civil rights era and the Vietnam War. I couldn't foresee how all-consuming the "Good Morning Show" would become, swallowing my life and that of my family in a whirling vortex of multi-dimensional experiences.

What else was I thinking that morning?"

I was extremely proud to be the host and executive producer of WFMY-TV'S "Good Morning Show." I was committed to making the experiment succeed. I was pumped. I had trained myself to be a good TV news reader. I had worked to soften my delivery and I was comfortable with the guy I was at that time. I knew I had the strength to work harder and longer than anyone else to make "my" program successful. In time the question of proprietorship would become one of the contentious problems buffeting the show, but in the beginning I was cooking on my own and loving it.

Viewers often inquire about my work schedule and the major question is, what time do I get up?

For the early shows I got up at 6 a.m. Later when we backed the sign on time down before dawn I got up as early as 3:30, 4:30, whenever I needed to get up.

Was I afraid of failing?

I was not victimized by a "fear of failure." I had devised a format and management had approved the concept. Since we had no idea how far we could expand the project given our resources it was an open-ended experiment. I was confident I could develop a show that would succeed if I controlled the content. Gaines Kelley wanted a product that would increase the station's revenue. The big question was, could the "Good Morning Show" make that happen? The cameraman was counting me down. With 15 seconds left I wished my viewers "the greatest day of their lives" promising "I'll be back Tuesday at 7:30 right here on WFMY-TV The Pied Piper of the Piedmont."

At 7:59 a.m. December 16, 1957, the first "Good Morning Show" was history.

TWO

In the Beginning

Early staff photo of Lee Kinard.

Broadcasting was a childhood infatuation. Since Mother put me to bed at dusk "with the chickens," the radio and books emerged as solacing diversions. They muffled the playful shouts of my wide-awake chums still rollicking in the vacant lot next door.

In the 1930s and '40s radio was a decent responsible medium delivering knowledge, information and entertainment. I enjoyed a diverse range of shows including "Inner Sanctum's" ghostly tales, quiz show competition on "Vox Jox," Saturday night's lineup of the week's top pops on the "Lucky Strike Hit Parade" and the fairy tales of "Let's Pretend."

The year 1939 was pivotal. In August my family visited the New York World's Fair's "World of Tomorrow," an exposition of innovative technologies and ideas destined to change the universe at mid-century. It promoted a medium called television that claimed to transmit pictures through the air! What a fantasy! Beyond the fair we toured Radio City Music Hall and watched live radio broadcasts at NBC. In Concord I drew the controls for my own radio console on the broad bottom of a cardboard box and broadcast from a corner of the basement.

The very next month Adolf Hitler spoiled our futuristic dreams with his distorted version of "The World of Tomorrow." When the Nazis' march into Poland launched World War II, much of the new technology showcased at the World's Fair was diverted to defend democracy. Now my bedside radio briefed me on the war as I grew from childhood to adolescence. The stars of CBS News, Ed Murrow, Bill Shirer, Eric Sevareid and Charles Collingwood, nurtured an embryonic infatuation with broadcast journalism. Sonorously guiding me across the Himalayan Mountains and Middle Eastern deserts, Lowell Thomas whetted a juvenile appetite for international travel. Battlefield reporter Ernie Pyle and public philosopher Walter Lippmann emerged as writing models. With their assignments, journeys and ideas these men mapped the mind of Lee Kinard.

I spoke into a radio microphone for the first time 50 years ago in the autumn of 1947. While studying at Woodrow Wilson High School in Beckley, West Virginia, I appeared on 29 weekly presentations of the "Youth Forum of the Air." The program was produced by our public speaking class and for students who lived in the "Soft Coal Capital of the World," the topics were controversial. We debated the "Taft-Hartly Law," "Strip Mining and Soil Conservation," and "Have the Morals of the American People Disintegrated?" Mind you, that was fifty years ago!

That high school experience marks the beginning of my broadcasting career. A spring Saturday morning a year or so later, back in North Carolina, I thumbed to Albemarle from nearby Pfeiffer College to seek fame and fortune at radio station WABZ. The 1,000-watt AM operation was licensed to broadcast from dawn to dusk. Confi-dent that experience on the youth forum and a winning record in public speaking were high qualifications, I set my sights on an announcing job.

My bravado wilted on the way to Albemarle. I prowled the town for an hour before I found the courage to walk into the station.

"What can I do for you, son?" Older than my mother, the receptionist sympathetically studied the sweaty, anxiety-stricken teenager trembling before her desk.

I stammered, "I'm here to apply for a job as a radio announcer!"

I couldn't tell whether she was silent from shock or straining to stifle a chuckle. After a long pause, I learned the station had just changed owner-ship.

"Our new general manager is due in the office any moment. Have a seat. Perhaps he'll have time to talk with you."

Half an hour later I met W.J. "Bill" Page, who would be my mentor, business partner and the best man at my wedding. Part of that was a few struggling years in the future, but to Bill's everlasting credit he gave me an immediate audition in his first five minutes as general manager of WABZ. On one of the busiest days of his life Bill Page literally gave a teenager a gift that would order the rest of his life.

I auditioned standing before a microphone in the station's single studio. The test included a commercial for the Donut Dinette, a news story and an obituary. Don't laugh! The ability to deliver a solemn, dignified obituary was significant since the daily "Obituary Column of the Air" was sponsored by a local funeral home. I survived the audition without flubbing or choking, but Page wasn't impressed.

"Kid, if you want to be a radio announcer it's going to take a lot of work, but if you want a job we need somebody to sweep and file records."

A few months later, much to Mother's displeasure I quit Pfeiffer College to janitor and "gofer" at WABZ for $13 a week. I stuck to the station like glue, waiting for one of the less ambitious announcers to get fired. When I got my big chance I booted it. I deeply offended Page's wife when I introduced a music selection by the eminent composer Frederick "Chop-ping," [Chopin] as in "chopping wood."

Page crushed me with a bitter ultimatum.

"Son, I'm afraid if you don't improve two hundred percent in two weeks I'm going to have to let you go."

I was devastated, but I was determined not to fail. I would prove to a deeply skeptical mother, and to myself, that dropping out of college wasn't a mistake. I took the station's wire recorder home to the attic I rented and practiced every moment I wasn't working. I doubt that I improved 200 percent but one of the remaining announcers was discovered dallying with a woman friend at the transmitter site and summarily fired. Thank heaven for engineers who get their wires crossed. I kept my job, but every day was a battle to survive. So, what else is new?

An unheated, uncooled attic is not the healthiest place to live. The winter of 1949-50 was a nightmare. When I was stricken with bronchitis, the Hotel Albemarle's manager took pity and rented me a room for a dollar a day. Since the radio studios were in the hotel basement I rode the elevator to work. The hotel dining room served inexpensive meals. The "Blue Plate Special," one meat, two vegetables, a roll and a drink cost $1.09. For a change in diet I occasionally bet the counter customers at Flave Whitley's Donut Dinette I could eat a dozen donuts if they would foot the bill.

In the summer of 1949, on a blind date, I met a kind and lovely young lady I immediately determined to marry. Anne Courtney Milton's good nature and friendship boosted my outlook on life and kept me from starving. Risking her mother's displeasure she often invited me to join her family for dinner. As my personal life broadened, more opportunities opened at the radio station. When Page said we needed a commercial writer I moved a typewriter into the control room. While the records played I pecked out commercials. By January, 1951, I was making $30 a week and buying clothes I wasn't ashamed to wear in public.

In 1952, when the station again went on the sales block, I was invited to purchase an equal 20 percent interest with Bill Page and three additional partners. A friendly banker loaned me $3,500 at two percent interest for the downpayment and overnight I was a radio station owner. Mother signed the papers because I was nearly a year shy of 21.

That fall, on Oct. 11, 1952, Anne and I were married. I had about $7 in my pocket when we set off that night on our honeymoon grand tour. The first night we got as far as Winston-Salem, and stayed at the Robert E. Lee Hotel, which later imploded but not, thank heavens, while we were there.

The next day we made it to a tourist cabin at Blowing Rock, and then we drove home by way of Hickory. We saw the sights and began a marriage that has lasted almost 45 years and given us three wonderful children, Beverly Ann, Valerie Grace and Lee Kinard III.

When I was summoned to active army duty a few months later, Anne worked and paid off our radio station loan and our first car.

Military service provided opportunities to work in television and film. I was a corporal at Ft. Bragg when the Army conducted its first atomic weapons maneuvers. I heard they needed someone to produce a film, called "Exercise Flashburn," which they would show to the top brass elsewhere. It was a great opportunity and I volunteered. And, as the only one with broadcast experience, I got the job, though I was also the only one on the team who was not a graduate of West Point. After that, I worked with Armed Forces Radio and TV, at Ft. McPherson, Georgia.

So when I came back to Albemarle I brought some new ideas. I wanted to expand our single station ownership into a chain of radio stations, but my partners were content with the status quo. Film and TV experience had generated more than a passing interest in those media. As I wrangled with my professional future, performing and producing on television seemed vastly more exciting than working in a small radio station.

Being invited to work at WFMY-TV was a thrilling experience. One Saturday in March, 1956, WFMY-TV Program Director Gomer Lesch came to Albemarle to check me out. After watching me disc-jockey for a couple of hours, Gomer invited me to Greensboro for a studio audition. I came to work at WFMY-TV as a staff announcer on Monday, April 16, 1956. Twenty

months to the day later the "Good Morning Show" premiered. Ironically, I recall telling Anne when we moved to Greensboro that we would probably be moving on after three years. I planned to learn the trade quickly and head to the "big time."

I hadn't counted on WFMY-TV's magnetism and powerful industry leadership. In 1947, the Jeffress family, owners of the Greensboro News Company, made a risky decision to diversify. Their first electronic project was an FM radio station. Their second courageous gamble was an application filed with the FCC for permission to operate a TV station. Putting a TV station on the air was a matter of all money and no return. In 1948, there were only 27 commercial TV stations on the air and most were operating deeply in the red. The Piedmont was fortunate to have entrepreneurs with the courage, cash and management savvy to invest in experimental and generally unprofitable electronic media.

The FM operation didn't succeed. But the TV station did. The Greensboro News Company squeezed TV equipment into the radio station's cramped quarters, and the first instant of live TV in the Carolinas occurred at 6:10 p.m. August 18, 1949, when Don Hardison introduced a four-and-a-half minute newscast. After a few frustrating false starts at getting Hardison's voice on the air, the first words viewers heard were the young announcer's exasperated "Judas Priest!"

It was the inauspicious birth of the 76th U.S. commercial station. Regular programming began for less than 2,000 sets in the Piedmont at 7 p.m. Thursday, September 22, 1949. The first broadcast day of three hours and five minutes marked the debut of the greatest community-oriented TV station in U.S. broadcasting history. Though I didn't have a clue at the time, it was the perfect match for a young broadcaster who was beginning to understand that being a part of a community was a dream far greater than the national fame I secretly coveted.

When I joined the staff in April, 1956, the station was telecasting from new state-of-the-art studios in northeastern Greensboro. A staff of more than 50 supported an 18-hour daily broadcast schedule. In 1997, almost that many work in the news department and WFMY-TV is on the air around the clock.

In the late '50s, Greensboro was entering a transitional phase, eventually affecting all of its 85,000-plus residents. New housing tracts and suburban shopping centers were beginning to tease customers away from the retailing giants along Elm Street. Belk, Meyers and Ellis-Stone department stores anchored the downtown. Schiffman's and Phipps Hardware provided elegant gifts for all occasions. The Carolina Theater was the city's movie palace. The S & W and Mayfair Cafeterias fed a steady stream of diners as did Meyer's Tea Room and the Woolworth lunch counter.

Downtown was really downtown, brighter and busier than Anne and Lee Kinard's smaller hometowns of Albemarle and Concord. We looked for opportunities to cruise Elm and Market Streets. At Christmas the business district, with its holiday window displays and bright lights was truly a magical place. Historically, this graying ambience was doomed by a changing America. A few years later, suburban flight and the 1960 Woolworth lunch counter sit-ins left downtown Greensboro a lonely beggar wandering.

I was still on a three-year track to learn TV and hit the highway to a major market when the opportunity to create a show of my own unfolded so simply that its promises were the dreams I fantasized. I had no inkling that a casual inquiry from Gomer Lesch would set the timetable for the remainder of my professional life. We were passing each other in the program lobby when Lesch stopped me.

"How'd you like to do a morning show?"

I didn't give the question a second's consideration. "I'd love it. What do you want me to do?"

He walked away. "I don't know. You figure it out and let me know what you'd like to do."

Years later I asked Gomer to recall his thoughts about the show. He replied:

"I cannot bring into focus a very specific recall of the idea for the program. My feeling is that we decided the local live show would be both competitive and a good community service opportunity, as well as a potentially valuable commercial property."

WFMY-TV was a CBS affiliate, but the network was struggling even then to develop an early morning concept. While CBS experimented with a variety of formats it failed to successfully compete with NBC's overwhelmingly popular "Today" hosted by Dave Garroway. In 1957 ABC-TV wasn't a morning player. The network didn't have an affiliate in the market and relied on WFMY-TV to telecast a selection of its programs.

I was still learning how to make material for TV, but I had years of experience producing and writing radio news and variety shows. "Filling time" was first a matter of making a format, the TV definition of an outline, and stacking it with certain kinds of information. I trusted I could qualify for this exceptional challenge and that Lesch would make my assignment happen. And he did.

"Your selection was simply a matter of the most appropriate personality for the effort. You have a pleasing personality, a good appearance and the kind of ad-lib capability that is needed on this type of program. I am sure we felt you were the obvious choice given the staff we had at that time, and given also some of the responsibilities of the other people. I don't believe we ever thought of anybody else for the spot."

The "Good Morning Show" did not begin as a "team" effort. Expeditiously, in that era WFMY-TV simply assigned a personality to simultaneously host and produce a show. Within broad guide lines those of us who hosted signature shows had nearly 100 percent control of our content, and therefore a degree of assumed ownership. We could make our shows in our images without being choked by a flock of "producers and assistant producers," or micro-managed.

If you wonder why I spent my career at WFMY-TV, there's your answer, control of content. I am firmly convinced that no producer anywhere has enjoyed the management confidence and support that I have for such a lengthy period. However, this is not to say that I have ever been foolish enough to take advantage of this trust, or that I have ignored the need or request to change. You can't survive 40 years in this business without changing.

The format I developed for the projected "Morning Show" was nothing more than an eight-page paste-up, school-type project. The handmade brochure's narrative was illustrated with cartoons scissored from a popular magazine then crudely typed and stapled. After 40 years the "pitch" is juvenile and rife with blatant exaggerations including the unconvincing line, "I like to get up in the morning!" Lesch was a man of at least a small amount of faith:

"Now here is a job that will offer a challenge. The Host of the 'Morning Show' will have to be on the ball to keep the show moving and to keep the viewer or the listener, as the case may be, interested in what's coming off. He should be wide awake, but not giddy, glib and soothing, at this time of the morning.

"I think, however, that by loading his little mind down with United Press chatter (a reference to newswire copy) and other tidbits, he will be able to keep the show moving at a steady pace without faltering too often. Here is one time in television when radio experience will pay off and I sincerely hope with pleasing results for all concerned.

"Frankly, I like to get up in the morning. I enjoy the chill of the crisp air, the smell of the Cone Mills Lake and the rubbish which litters the highway on my way to work. The taste of old cigarettes, the weird aroma of Studio One after the air conditioner blowers have been off all night and the burning, sickly sensation of the first cup of Nescafe in a melting paper cup from the kitchen. These are just a few reasons why I think Lee Kinard is the man for the 'Morning Show.'

At 7:59:30, December 16, 1957, the first show was over. We got on and off on time. In pioneering days that's how we often measured success. The show and Lee Kinard had become Siamese twins, co-joined, inseparable. When I breathed it breathed. Nobody was waiting in the wings to tell me what a great job I had done. Accolades weren't easy to come by in those days. You couldn't even post credits for a show unless you had management approval.

The major crisis of infancy was motivating the show's director to come to work on time! A second desperate need was video to cover the two to three records we played each morning. Program Director Jack Markham, who succeeded Gomer Lesch recalled: "We thought we were being very innovative if we could figure out some video to show during a record. We would even show a control room turntable with a record spinning on it from time to time."

We used all sorts of material for those "Stone-Age music videos" including excerpts from the station's collection of theater cartoons. I remember the camera tracking a roach winding its way across the studio while Harry James trumpeted "Crazy Rhythm."

For a long, long time we programmed shoppers' video over the records. Our photographers hung out in the coverage area filming pedestrians in the Piedmont's various downtowns. Filmed from the rear the bobbing buttocks of these unaware shoppers raised hilarious hoots from the studio crew. We built a hand puppet theater into our set and viewers gasped in amazement as white gloved hands mixed volatile chemical potions that erupted in clouds of smoke and near fatal vapors.

WFMY-TV was committed to establishing the "Good Morning Show" as a revenue source for the station, but the show premiered without a single commercial. Creating sales credibility was going to be an uphill battle. In the weeks ahead we would devise various strategies to raise the program's commercial appeal. In time the "Good Morning Show" built a huge audience, but for far too long the show was marketed at "Blue Light Special" rates to attract local businesses to TV. When the commercials achieved major results, which they often did, advertisers were coaxed into more expensive contracts in the evening and late news.

The "Good Morning Show" has never been blessed with a definitive line-item budget, but maybe that's been the show's salvation. The only limits were consensus parameters. For that reason you could often find me in the front office pleading my case for additional resources, but then those who produce local TV are accustomed to intensive lawyering. We spend a lot of hours before the bar.

Next, "Success on a shoestring!" as "The Good Morning Show" continues—after this pause on WFMY-TV, The Pied Piper of the Piedmont.

THREE

Growing Up in Local TV

Lee Kinard on the set. According to Lee, in time the clock became the show's number one attraction.

Hang on! In this chapter I'm going to fly you across the mystifying, tumultuous '60s and '70s. You'll encounter a whole series of changes triggered by historical events, competition, management decisions and co-hosts. Many of the program's encounters deserve more definitive chapters. The civil rights era, the co-hosts, the weather emergencies and the travel stories will come later. You'll learn why and how the "Good Morning Show" evolved and expanded during a turbulent period in American history.

In 1957, the "Good Morning Show" was a radio show on TV telecast in black and white with few visuals and rudimentary graphics. We exploited our curiosity and spontaneity to produce content. Lacking "theoretical" knowledge we tested experimental ideas on the air. As the sole producer, I presented the news content I believed my viewers needed to know. The decorous approach to what I delivered was based on the "common sense philosophy" of my "raising." If certain stories offended me I didn't read them. When personally repelled, I ignored socially volatile stories, particularly those dealing with the despised Ku Klux Klan.

I speak for myself because WFMY-TV operated without a professional news director for some years. Even I held that responsibility for a few weeks. Based on our primitive technical capabilities a lot of thought went into what we should and could report as local news. Early on we did not have reporters per se on the staff and many stories we might have covered seemed better served by print media.

Consciously, I was a serious gatekeeper. Sub-consciously, I didn't have the slightest idea what the political implications of that strategy could mean to an audience. Those of us charged with delivering the news had experienced World War II, the Korean

War and the beginning of the Cold War. By comparison, local news paled. Besides, TV was a major new medium. Why contaminate its virginal vaudevillian aura with the mundane and miserable?

Three major events, the civil rights era, the women's liberation movement and the Vietnam War transformed WFMY-TV and its staff announcers into anchors, reporters and pseudo-social scientists. More about that later. But first, what did you see when you watched the "Good Morning Show" in the '60s and '70s? The answer is a whole lot of Lee Kinard. We began producing substantially entertaining field features when Greensboro native John Black assumed the show's directorial duties.

The material Black produced and edited with legendary photographers Buddy Moore and Bill Gordon dramatically enlarged the character of the show. Black helped us get "on the road" and out into the Piedmont with filmed series on historical homes and battle-fields. His creative efforts set the tone for most of the directors who succeeded him.

Few people have ever been assigned full-time to the "Good Morning Show," and that includes me. Most of us have had other duties so we scavenged ideas and talent. If anybody on the studio crew had an idea to improve the show I generally okayed a trial run. That is as true today as it was 40 years ago. Many of our innovators were highly-motivated production assistants.

We threw ideas on the screen and waited to see if they breathed. Because we weren't hamstrung by unions and supervisors, talented staff from any department could actively capitalize on periods of creativity without being hindered by meddling producers. We made variety, created vaudeville, shaped the medium as we matured.

We quickly discovered that live TV was a gluttonous monster that sucked up ideas like a vacuum cleaner, but it was our life and God it was great! It took time and effort to take a camera into the field, write and edit a feature, but the company paid overtime and we needed cash to nourish our families. So, we ignored the wife and kids and soaked up the "OT" for Santa Claus and the weekly grocery bill.

When the first ratings arrived, we knew the size of the challenge we faced if the "Good Morning Show" were to succeed. In April, 1958, the show posted an Arbitron Metro rating of 2 in Guilford and Forsyth counties. The fact that we were reaching only a mere two percent of all the television sets in the area stirred a scary scenario. It was not a positive number. For our primitive marketing strategy we decided to buy an audience with a ridiculous "Mystery Personality Contest."

This lottery-like contrivance offered inexpensive prizes to viewers who correctly identified a thinly-disguised TV personality and mailed their answers to the "Good Morning Show." Each Friday three prize winners were drawn from the week's mail and awarded small electrical appliances. When responses poured in at the rate of 3,000-5,000 a week for a chance to win electric toasters, waffle makers, blenders, knives and irons we considered ourselves marketing geniuses. Plus the postmarks told us who was watching and where they lived, mapping our strengths and weaknesses.

This promotional scheme never cost more than $30 a week. It was an economical strategy to build an audience in an era when "the more electricity you used the less it cost." By March, 1959, our rating had soared to nearly eight percent and we were drawing mail from more than 100 Piedmont cities and towns. The "Mystery Personality Contest" established the "Good

Sometimes the Mystery Personality Contest winners would be drawn by celebrities such as Hugh O'Brien, shown here with Lee.

Morning Show" as a productive advertising medium.

The 1960s began with talk about the pill and payola. We groped for felt-tip pens and boiled with Teflon cookware. The Soviets shot down Gary Powers' U-2 spy plane, then one of our RB 47s over the Arctic. The Gross National Product totaled $503 billion making 1960 the most productive year in American history. However, before the decade ended viewers would find themselves facing an escalating conflict in Southeast Asia and a social earthquake that threatened to shatter America.

The first major national event to hit the show exploded the human relations status quo in Greensboro on February 1, 1960. The city became an international headline when four students from N.C. A&T State University seated themselves at the downtown Woolworth's whites-only lunch counter and refused to leave. Within a few days we knew the civil rights era was here to stay. As this first episode in a relentless war against prejudice developed, I asked management for guidance. What role should the "Good Morning

Show" play during this critical period?

I was instructed to position the program as a positive community mirror. The top-story sit-ins were covered during regularly-scheduled "Good Morning Show" newscasts while segments within the body of the show were devoted to issues and features reinforcing civility and the status quo. At this point in its early history the "Good Morning Show" did not become, as it did later, a forum for the discussion of racial issues.

Paradoxically, the beginning of the civil rights movement paralleled the

Kinard and Chief Photographer Buddy Moore searching for Blockade Runners off Carolina Beach.

Centennial Commemoration of the Civil War 1960-65. For five years I wrote and produced a daily five-minute chronological flashback summary of the conflict. Many topics were filmed on location in Manassas, Gettysburg and Richmond-Petersburg. One of my most exciting series highlighted the recovery of artifacts from the wrecks of sunken Civil War blockade runners off Carolina Beach.

In the frenzied, questioning '60s "Age of Aquarius" the "Good Morning Show" explored pop culture's infatuations. The renowned Duke University-based parapsychologist Dr. J.B. Rhine, his wife Louisa, and many of his colleagues provided material for our extensive investigation of extra-sensory perception. As a counter-balance for bad news the "Good Morning Show" became a variety show. Our inspirational devotional hymn was presented by Alamance County tenor Bill Kirkpatrick. The Willis Sisters, an attractive talented trio from Danville, Virginia, added popular music to a format that showcased gospel and country and western tunes. Departing from the concept of a radio show on TV we produced a more visual, whimsically entertaining TV show.

In the mid '60s, the Jeffress family sold The Greensboro News Company and WFMY-TV to Landmark Communications. Following the transaction rumors of impending challenges to our federal broadcast license renewal by citizen groups encouraged General Manager William A. Gietz to frame a new mission for the "Good Morning Show." In addition to weather, news and sports we would henceforth commit 25 minutes a day to community public service information.

Overnight the "Good Morning Show" evolved into a studio-originated public affairs talk show, a mission that would dominate the content for 15 years. Bonding with our various Piedmont communities we welcomed guests from area chambers of commerce, United Way organizations, human service agencies, disease foundations, schools and colleges. For all practical purposes the "Good Morning Show" became the Piedmont's public access channel.

In 1971 when Greensboro's public schools desegregated, the program

Lee accepting the School Bell Award from William Daniels. WFMY has received several educational awards.

accepted a major leadership role in sustaining civil harmony in the community. To assist compliance with the judicial mandate, we introduced a daily "School Days" segment. While exploring a variety of topics to insure viewers that public schools were operating safely and soundly, we created a national model, a prototype public relations venture, for the growing emphasis on school-community relations. The North Carolina Association of Educators recognized "School Days" with six coveted "School Bell Awards."

Desegregation was implemented through massive busing, assigning thousands of students to ride buses earlier to class. The "Good Morning Show" moved back its sign-on from 6:30 to 6 a.m. to accommodate our viewers. With thousands of school buses now moving through the Piedmont, pertinent weather information assumed a more dramatic importance. The program became the major regional source for "snow desk" emergency information. As the "only show in town" ours often was the channel for that final word on whether winter storms would close schools for tens of thousands of Piedmont children. Ask long time Piedmont residents about their first memories of the "Good Morning Show" and they are likely to reply, "I remember waiting for Lee Kinard to tell me I didn't have to go to school."

During the '60s and '70s we made familiar faces stars. One of our most popular guests was the persistent North Carolina UFO investigator George Fawcett, an outer space sleuth who tracked and reported every suspicioned UFO. We innovated health features before they became voguish, utilizing the dietary expertise of

Greensboro Seventh Day Adventist Pastor Paul Dixon and his wife Becky. This extensive series on diet and non-smoking pre-dated the healthy lifestyle series viewers commend us for in the 90s.

The "Good Morning Show" franchised fitness before it became chic, with our personal trainer Jane Sharp, a mainstay at the Greensboro YWCA, who offered daily exercises. Personable artist Jill Troutman first appeared on April 10, 1974 painting, herself into a lifestyle transformation by originating huge gaudy flowers on canvas with gobs of toilet paper. Greensboro psychologist Dr. John Edwards represented the Greensboro Family Life Council one morning and came back regularly for more than a quarter century.

In the mid '70s the "Good Morning Show" was attracting seven percent of early morning viewers and staying ahead of our competitors. That's when many of them were trooping off to the movies to see "Jaws" chew up sailors, swimmers and boats. More than a million divorces a year were reported in the U.S. In April 1975 helicopters lifted the last known Americans out of Vietnam and the South Vietnamese government surrendered. Buttons and bumper stickers read: THANKS MOM FOR NOT HAVING AN ABORTION.

In 1975 Landmark Communications of Norfolk sold WFMY-TV to Harte-Hanks Communications, Inc. of San Antonio, Texas. We joined a TV Group managed by Wayne Kearl that included stations in San Antonio, Texas, Springfield, Missouri, and Jacksonville, Florida. Wayne was a great supporter of the "Good Morning Show:"

"When we were first looking at WFMY-TV as prospective purchasers, I was quite surprised to find a two-hour morning show on a local live basis. It turned out to be a happy surprise! I learned from my ascertainment interviews how warmly the public regards the "Good Morning Show." And I myself immediately liked your pleasant, low-key approach, and the rich sense of community you convey. It's a distinguished program, a significant service to the community, that you and WFMY-TV can take great pride in."

• • •

Wow! A monumental change!

In the autumn of 1976 a fading "Captain Kangaroo" was bumped from his 8 a.m. slot and the "Good Morning Show" expanded to three hours (6-9 a.m.). The third hour was titled "Good Morning Times Two" and showcased the program's first female and African-American co-host Sandra Hughes. These were troubled years when many Piedmont viewers were still struggling to accept African-Americans on TV. Sandra's afternoon talk show had been disrupted time and again by bomb threats, warning us to expect the worst when "Good Morning Times Two" premiered. Both Sandra and I felt we had been precariously paired. As she said:

"When I had the opportunity to do GMTT with you (Lee), then that gave me a chance to expand what I considered talents I might have, or do something that people didn't expect me to do; to sit with you on the morning show, with a person who obviously had already developed star potential, in my opinion elevated me. I remember it as being a confusing experience, number one because we had so many things we had to do. I considered it second-ary to the other things I was doing. It did not take a high priority in my opinion with the kinds of responsibilities ("Sandra and Friends," 1-1:30 p.m.) that I had. I remember worrying about whether you were comfortable with me working with you."

I didn't know Sandra well but I respected her as a person and as a professional. I had no personal qualms about working with her, but there were many people who thought that the pairing was detrimental to my career and the "Good Morning Show." My concern lay with our chemistry, the behavioral properties that define an elusive quality of respect, truth and comfort that germinates in a non-threatening setting. On TV we had to approach each other sincerely and decorously while appearing artfully casual. We were an African-American female and a White Anglo-Saxon male breaking new ground in the mid-South. At best, relationships of this caliber had a volatile history.

In extemporaneous conversation, happy talk repartee, we needed to communicate so that neither was diminished and each personality was enhanced. We were two performers from two different worlds. We had to be models and we had no models to study. From the beginning we were successful because of mutual trust, respect and a dual determination to make our teaming work.

Producing this three-hour format turned out to be a living, bleeding nightmare. I have never been involved in an innovative project on such a tremendous scale. The "Good Morning Show-Good Morning Times Two" of that era should not be confused with contemporary "news wheels" that indulge in repetitive programming. We staged huge TV specials including "Bake-Off" cooking competitions on the Pillsbury model. We filmed intricately-produced features on location including a major Christmas program from Chinqua-Penn Plantation near Reidsville. We produced a poetry roundtable spotlighting the region's foremost published authors. We provided hints to solve every household crisis imaginable in 15 hours of TV time per week. No single person involved worked full time on the show. We all had multiple responsibilities beyond the morning madness.

I cheered the loudest when "Good Morning Times Two" was cancelled following the February 1977 sweeps. It was not a question of poor ratings, or objection to black and white hosts. The fast-paced three-hour circus was exhausting the crew. We didn't have the luxury of the syndicated packages producers fill time with today and we did not have the "live" capabilities we have in 1997. I hyperventilated from the show's inception until its cancellation, but Sandra reacted to the loss in a more painful manner:

"Once we got going with the show, I had a feeling we were going to turn it into something regardless of my initial feelings. I was very disappointed when, after a few months, they took it off the air. I didn't feel the station had given it a chance to grow and become what it could (become). Another reason I think I felt that way is because I've always been the kind of person that when you give me something, even though it's more than I need or want, don't take it back from me—that is the way I felt about that show. I felt that something had been taken away from me."

At best "Good Morning Times Two" was a tedious, laborious, mystifying, exhausting task. Perhaps we shot ourselves in the feet because we were overly ambitious, or because management was unreasonable in its expectations. We cared about the show, we adopted it as a personal challenge, and while it traumatized us it didn't affect the ratings as the "Good Morning Show" began its 20th year in a relatively strong position:

Program/station	Rating	Homes
GMS/WFMY	7	28,000
GMAmerica/WGHP	3	12,000
Today/WXII	5	21,000

When interviewers ask what propelled the "Good Morning Show" into the number-one position in the Piedmont viewing mix in the '60s and '70s I am quick to reply "the weather!" Having alluded to our "Snow Desk" promotion I'd like to expand on some of our more harrowing, icy adventures in the next episode. So, if you're ready to skid and slide along with me, let's keep the '60s and '70s in gear and grind our way into a flurry of new episodic adventures on the "Good Morning Show."

FOUR

Foul Weather Friends

Lee forecasting the weather in the 1970s. In 40 years, weathermaps evolved from paper to felt, then projected 33mm slides, to computer- generated graphics.

You're Lee Kinard! Man, I loved you when I was a kid in school and you came on TV those snowy mornings and told us that the Alamance County Schools have cancelled classes for today!

I've heard similar reminiscences from viewers in every hamlet, village, town and city in the Piedmont. If you don't live in the region and aren't familiar with the realm's cultural personality it may be difficult for you to comprehend why snow is a phenomenal experience transforming us into flaky, fluttering dervishes. A mere rumor of snow triggers a carnival-like atmosphere. People rush to supermarkets and lay in huge stocks of milk, bread, baby food and various categories of siege supplies. As a long- time resident I can state unequivocally, from personal and observational experience, that most of us are still attempting to master the art of driving in snow and ice.

Factually, viewers know Lee Kinard despises snow. Oh sure, as a kid I loved it until I busted my face sledding down an icy hill. When I was a teenager living in Beckley, West Virginia, it was my before-dawn task to dig glutinous coal from a frozen mound to feed the potbellied stove that barely kept us alive on the ice-sheeted Appalachian plateau.

When I began the "Good Morning Show," I didn't know diddley-squat about meteorology. My major weather experience involved hurricane coverage as a reporter for an Armed Forces radio station in San Juan, Puerto Rico. Most of my weather knowledge was initially gleaned from the pages of my children's encyclopedia. The first time I substituted on the evening weather at WFMY-TV I managed to fill two minutes of the four allotted. But I did make the effort to learn something about forecasting. I consulted J. P. Molen, the first

National Weather Service meteorologist assigned to the old Greensboro-High Point Weather Station. Then, as the years piled up I drew on my experience to predict on the basis of past weather system performances. Most of the time I stuck with the National Weather Service forecasts and I loved it when they started adding probabilities to the outlook. That erased a lot of pressure.

The Piedmont region of Virginia, North and South Carolina is one of the most difficult areas in the U.S. to forecast. The predictable variance between snow and ice is based on several critical factors including a solid wedge of high pressure cold air over Pennsylvania interacting with a soggy low pressure system moving across central South Carolina. But the crucial factor determining ice, sleet, snow or freezing rain is the temperature of the air at the various levels of the atmosphere. Until radar and satellite pictures became available, forecasters had to rely on previously-recorded data and observational stations that were seldom in the right place at the right time.

There were always threats to my accuracy from the west. The Appalachians often blocked or delayed weather systems moving southeastward from the northern plains. Since the only National Weather Service radar station was located on the western slope of the Appalachians I often didn't know what kind of precipitation we would get until it started falling. I danced precariously through all my winter weather forecasts pointing out factor after factor that could vary any prediction.

At times it was an onerous task just to forecast sunny skies. People associate sunshine with high pressure systems, but even highs can't cope with northeasterly winds that roll up against the side of the Appalachians and fold the moisture back across the Piedmont like a wet blanket. These systems are often as stubborn as a southern mule and hang on for days.

The first forecasts on the "Good Morning Show" were simply that, forecasts. In the beginning we did not use a weather map, and of course we didn't have any of the technological bells and whistles our "News 2" meteorologists feature on their segments. Since snow was "the" event that established the "Good Morning Show" as a major information source let's relive a few snow days.

During the first "Good Morning Show" years we didn't take snow seriously. Before it became popular to assume the mantle of "journalists" we reacted to snow like kids. The crew pushed a studio camera to the door and shot our snowball fights in the parking lot. Yes, it was a less frenetic world, but in this case television didn't change society; nature bent the emphasis toward bigger and better weathercasts.

Forty years ago there were no interstates, less business commuting and fewer school buses. Rural students were generally bused, but in the towns and cities most kids walked to neighborhood schools. Prior to 1960, WFMY-TV's management was more concerned about the fate of birds than the general public. It was a standing joke that our major mission in the event of a snowstorm was to encourage our viewers to "feed the birds." General Manager Gaines Kelley issued a memo to that effect.

Three snarling snowstorms on suc-cessive Wednesdays in March, 1960, dramatically changed the Piedmont's perception of wintertime. The resulting chaotic disruptions fostered by nearly 22 inches of snow spurred the "Good Morning Show" to engage all available resources to provide the public with emergency information. In that hectic month the "Good Morning Show's" snow desk gained a regional reputation as the community weather-watch headquarters. Snow made the "Good Morning Show" into a household viewing habit to the extent that we began to pray for weather anomalies during the winter sweeps period.

While weather emergencies may have boosted our ratings and reputation as a public servant, snow and ice created multiple problems for the program's staff. First and foremost we had to get to work before everybody else. For many, many years WFMY-TV did not provide emergency inclement weather transportation for its employees. Now, this may not seem like a big deal today when all-purpose vehicles, four-wheel drive, and radial tires are the norm, but, by golly, 30 years ago snow and ice triggered panic in the Kinard household.

I bought my first four-wheel drive vehicle in 1984. Until then I made do with a disreputable series of clunkers. Most of the time I had my hands full paying for recaps. Snow and ice storms always caught me riding the last half-mile out of bald eagles and unable to get to a service station to have chains installed. When my tires were slick and I was trapped at the house I walked to work or imposed on fellow workers to give me a ride. Former "Good Morning Show" Director John Black remembers one anxious morning when the ride didn't happen:

"One morning we awoke to a city covered with snow. Dave Wright (11 p.m. weatherman) had said only a few flakes would fall. Well, Herb Clark, our engineer, drove his old Kaiser-Frazier auto to your house to pick you up. When he didn't see any lights on, he figured you had gone on to the station on your own. As he drove off, you came out of the door and watched him disappear down the street. I don't recall how you got to the station that day, but I remember how nervous I got thinking I would have to do the show myself.

However, you made it just in time and my shaking hands settled down a bit."

I walked to work that morning and on similar occasions for more than a quarter-century. From the mid-to-late '60s we lived in a remote suburban development 10 miles from the studio. One bitter morning Anne stood crying at the door as I set out in a blinding snowstorm at 1:30 a.m. The first two miles took me down a dark county road through a forest, across a small stream and up a hill. Blowing and drifting snow made it difficult to figure out where the roadbed began and ended with a descent into deep side ditches.

Since Cone Boulevard did not yet link northwestern and northeastern Greensboro I had to get to downtown Greensboro before I could turn northeastward toward the studios at the intersection of Phillips Avenue and White Street. After toiling through drifts for almost five hours I staggered into Studio One minutes before sign on. How big a deal was this? Well, if I hadn't shown up they would have rolled a standby film feature. Again I was the entire show, the pitcher and the catcher, I played all the bases and umpired.

Today, in a world where people can't imagine crossing the street without driving, viewers are amazed that I actually walked to work. I loved my show and my audience. When I saw how bad weather could paralyze our neighborhoods I made up my mind to shepherd my flock come rain, sleet or snow. The integration of the Greensboro public schools and massive busing created even more threatening situations. With hundreds of new buses traversing city streets, winter weather emerged as an even greater threat to our children's safety. The first pickups occurring as early as 6:45 influenced my decision to roll our sign-on back from 6:30 to 6 a.m.

During this period I often consulted with the Greensboro public schools when severe weather threatened. For a few years on occasion I was at least partially responsible for dismissing thousands of students. When other school systems, businesses and institutions discovered the "Good Morning Show's" Snow Desk services a demand for emergency announcements escalated dramatically until they were flowing in by the hundreds.

We began by reading them on the air as often as possible. We read and read and read until we finally attained the computer technology to organize and program the messages alphabetically by categories. But, the constant reading was exhilarating coverage of a great region-impacting news story. Some mornings I'd grab a stool and drag it outside with a cup of coffee and read the closings in the blizzard. When an action shot was warranted the camera zoomed past me to scan cars sliding through the intersection of Phillips Avenue and White Street.

I pray I never see the recurrence of one icy morning. It was a marginal situation when we couldn't specifically predict snow or freezing rain. Shortly after 6:30 a.m. the temperature began to fall steadily. When it reached 27 degrees our roads began icing. By this time thousands of buses loaded with students were criss-crossing the quickly-icing Piedmont. School transportation systems called in panic, "Tell your viewers to go into the streets to stop the buses where they are!," they demanded.

That scared the dickens out of me. I went on the air begging folks to hail and hold the buses in their neighborhoods.

"Tell the drivers to stop where they are until we figure out how long this freezing rain is going to last," I pleaded. I imagined the worst as I choked back the tears. It was an awful experience.

Today snowy-icy days are a bigger pain in the neck than ever. We have "Snow Codes" that school systems, institutions and eligible businesses can apply for that assure them a free spot on our computerized "crawl." The problem is that some mornings we have 1,200 messages in the computer. If someone calls with a new message in the midst of the crawl it takes 40 minutes for the announcement to appear on the screen. We have been forced to plead with the audiences we have desperately recruited to organize their own emergency systems.

Weather caused me to miss the only "Good Morning Show" of my career. One extremely foggy morning I drove to work using the curbing on the right-hand side of the road as a guide. At 35 miles per hour I didn't see the intersection where Cone Boulevard dead-ended until it was too late. The next instant I found myself plunging into a side ditch-like abyss. Fortunately a passerby witnessed the crash and helped me evacuate the wreck.

The police found me standing in the road bleeding from the mouth. They were immediately more interested in what I was doing driving around at four in the morning than the extent of my injuries. Later, in the emergency room as the surgeon sewed my face into one piece, one of the cops looked down through the surgical lights to reassure me I wouldn't be charged with careless and reckless driving!

Today's "Good Morning Show" weather is presented by "News 2" meteorologist Ed Matthews. Eddie is one of the most conscientious professionals I have had the pleasure of working with, a man who takes the weather and our viewers' safety seriously. He has the complete confidence of "News 2" meteorologist Randy Jackson and the entire "Good Morning Show" staff.

Sometimes it's rewarding to "give up" something you've done for a long, long time. In my career I've passed a lot of those mileposts and there isn't one I've regretted. When Matthews became our meteorologist he took a huge burden off my shoulders and added a whole new dimension to our program. I guess by now you've figured out that I am extremely proud of the standard the "Good Morning Show" sets for weather reporting in the Piedmont. It's one "dance" I don't have to do anymore. More about that after this pause for station identification.

This set in the 1970s commemorated WFMY's 20th anniversary.

FIVE

Celebrity Spotlight

Jayne Mansfield was a tremendous hit with WFMY's audience while playing
Greensboro's Plantation Supper Club in 1963.

The question about the "Good Morning Show" that is most difficult to answer is, "Who is the most famous person to ever visit the program?" Well, we haven't hosted the President or the Vice President, but we have welcomed Queen Sirikit of Thailand, dozens of congressmen, senators, governors, and hundreds of celebrities. We introduced North Carolina's first-ever Miss America, Asheville's Maria Beale Fletcher, and Graham's Jeanne Swanner, the tallest-ever Miss America contestant and winner of the Miss Congeniality Award.

For reasons both romantic and tragic the celebrity that comes first to memory is Jayne Mansfield. Mansfield's relationship with the "Good Morning Show" says more about her real character than much of what has been written and dramatized on TV. More than just a glitzy, glamorous, vacuous blonde, she could be the "girl next door," an attentive mother, an affectionate wife, whose physical attributes provided an entree into show business. Mansfield's movie career was fading when she played Fred Koury's Plantation Supper Club. I interviewed her at a press party promoting her cabaret act, but I actually spent more time talking off camera with her husband Mickey Hargitay.

The Hungarian body-builder muscled himself to celebrity status in Hollywood in an era when the body-building, fitness craze was bulging at the sinews but had not yet expanded beyond California. I asked Mickey if he would enjoy demonstrating some of his exercises on the "Good Morning Show." "Yes," emerged quickly in a rich Balkan accent.

Chief Photographer Buddy Moore volunteered to drive Hargitay to the station the following morning and therein lies a gem of a story! The way Moore told it, when he buzzed the Hargitays' Plantation Motel room, Jayne and her son Zoltan came tripping out with Mickey. The Hargitays had apparently decided to entertain the "Good Morning Show" audience with a family routine. Of course it never entered my mind that Mansfield would get out of the sack to make a 7:30 a.m. local TV show, but wow! She did.

Check this! On the way to the studio Mansfield asked Moore to stop at the TV Grill, a popular breakfast spot across the street from WFMY-TV. Jayne bounced out of the car and pranced into one of Greensboro's finest working-class diners. When this stunningly attractive, gorgeously endowed Hollywood siren sauntered to the counter and ordered "orange juice to go" her appearance sucked the sound out of the raucous crowd. It's a miracle there weren't a few strokes among the breakfasting mechanics, carpenters, plumbers and garbage truck drivers. Cameraman Moore was so floored by Mansfield's move he didn't have presence of mind to grab his camera and film the incident.

I can't criticize Buddy for zoning out because I was equally shocked when Mansfield towed Zoltan and Mickey into the studio in the middle of my weather report. The fact that she was sleepy-eyed made her all the more sensual. The first question that popped in my mind was, would she exercise with Mickey? I knew I was looking at one of those "moments" every live TV show producer lives for!

Yes! Yes! Yes! They would do a family routine! I introduced them to the audience, bantered briefly, prompting Jayne to describe her cabaret act at the Plantation and then turned the show over to Mickey. Mansfield may have been a dimming nova but her friendly attitude drew an audience of young mothers from the residential development adjacent to the station. They waited for Jayne in the lobby, pregnant, barefooted, babies at breast and in tow, pleading for autographs which she graciously provided.

Sadly, Jayne Mansfield's story doesn't have a happy ending. One morning while collecting facsimile photographs for the "Good Morning Show" newscasts I came across a series of shocking pictures snapped a few hours previously on a dark Louisiana road. They documented the fatal automobile accident that decapitated Jayne Mansfield. One shocking picture showed her severed head plopped on the hood of the death vehicle. I have never been able to completely erase that macabre image from my memory. I hope that somewhere along her brief journey she enjoyed an abundance of happiness, but in memoriam she and Mickey Hargitay certainly brightened one "Good Morning Show."

One of our most popular celebrity guests is Eileen Fulton, the voluptuous Lisa of the CBS soap "As The World Turns." The daughter of a Methodist minister who served several congregations in North Carolina, Eileen returns regularly to the Piedmont to support projects at her alma mater Greensboro College. She's invited me to make a cameo appearance on "As The World Turns," but I've never been able to muster the courage to let her "vamp" me.

Most of the film and TV stars who guested on the "Good Morning Show" appeared live in the '60s and '70s before satellite technology made it more convenient for them to sit in a New York studio and reel off interviews without leaving the city. Those we were fortunate to interview were playing the popular dinner theater circuit. North Carolina's Shepherd Strudwick was one of our very first guests. Jeanne Crain stopped by and left a hanky as a momento. A few dozen years after vocalist Eddie Fisher visited, his former wife Debbie Reynolds showed her appreciation for our chat with a kiss. That was a moment I've archived on videotape.

During this same period CBS staged "star junkets" in Washington, D.C., Atlanta and Hollywood. Interviewing stars in a hotel suite wasn't exactly like having them in your own studio but I met some great names, including Larry Hagman, the inimitable J.R. Ewing. I was having a cup of coffee and chatting with my counterpart from a Cincinnati station when Larry Hagman arrived at our suite for his interview. At that point he had filmed the first four episodes of "Dallas." We congratulated him on what appeared to be the beginning of a successful new series, but Hagman wanted to grouse about the frustrations of show business and the downside of stardom.

According to Hagman, after "I Dream of Jeannie" (NBC 1965-69) ended its network run his agent couldn't find him a job in the industry. Larry didn't mince any words about the depth of his frustration: "My agent would call up and offer me to some producer and the guy would reply, 'Hagman? Who wants that 'old fart.'" On the brink of monumental success with "Dallas" he was bitter because "Jeannie" re-runs playing successfully all over the country didn't pay him a dime in residuals. Hagman deserved every buck he made off "Dallas" and I hope he's getting residuals to pay for his new liver.

During the "Dallas" run I interviewed Larry at least three times. The longer he played J.R. the more he became J.R. He was a tough cookie. The first time I sat down to talk with him he wanted to know if I smoked. I didn't, but he wasn't impressed. During the entire interview he held a battery-operated fan in his lap blowing cool air across his face. It distracted me and he took advantage of my discomfort, but I never let him forget it. By the way, Hagman's mother, Mary Martin, was a gracious lady whose autograph I have on a Fieldcrest pillowcase, a memento from an interview taped for the "Good Morning Show" at the Fieldcrest-Cannon Store in Eden.

Through the years I interviewed Sebastian Cabot, John Forsythe, William and Robert Conrad, the entire cast from "Mash," Ed Asner, Cloris Leachman, Will Geer, Leonard Nimoy, Hugh O'Brien and Mike Connors. I enjoyed a marvelous conversation with ebullient Pearl Bailey who graciously honored me with signed copies of all her books. My toughest interviews were Carroll O'Connor, during his Archie Bunker years, and Mary Tyler Moore, after she had ditched the lovable "Mary Tyler Moore Show." I probably interviewed 90 percent of the CBS-TV stars during the '60s and '70s and most of them were swell people.

Flip the coin and stand back. Here comes Richard Simmons, the world's wackiest fitness master. Simmons has been on the show more times than I've invited him. He invites himself. Richard Simmons is a maniac. On his first appearance he didn't wait for an introduction. He barged through the lobby, overwhelmed security, blasted into the studio, raced onto the living room set, picked me up and hugged me. He was rancid to a degree from sprinting through the studio.

"Richard, don't kiss me. Please put me down!"

Richard's impromptu explosion would have been a great teaser for our seven o'clock hour, but he wouldn't get off the set. Totally out of control he took over the show. Twenty minutes later we still hadn't broadcast any weather, news or sports. I was going through one of those periods when I was super-sensitive to management's opinion of the "Good Morning Show" and I fully expected the news director to come whining about a major deviation from the format. But nobody complained, at least to my face.

We've tried every trick in the book to discourage Richard from destroying the show but he keeps showing up. Finally, we learned to control him by staging his limo arrival and walk down to the studio as an on-camera event. At least we know when he is going to burst through the studio doors. We really set the prankster up for his 1996 visit. Thank heaven his annual haunting of the Piedmont coincided with my assignment in France. Richard didn't know I was out of the country. When he arrived in the studio the only Lee Kinard to greet him was a life-size cutout. The little butterball was crushed! Yes!

Director Laura Murray rolled a video tape greeting from me that said something like: "Richard, I really can't tell you how sorry I am that I am not in Greensboro to greet you in person. Sadly, I have been sent to Paris on a special assignment and, Richard, that assignment is to interview—Barbara Striesand!"

If you know anything about Richard Simmons you know that he fantasizes about meeting Streisand. Every network host he appears with taunts him with promises of Barbara's appearance which never materializes. The report I received said Richard went berserk. He grabbed my wireless microphone and jammed it down in his shorts, pretty gross for even Richard. He babbled, whined and accused me of devious crimes. I was elated to miss Richard's appearance and I swear if he ever gets booked for the show again

I'll call in sick, or plan another trip to France.

That's a joke.

I salute Richard Simmons for the lives he has saved and the love he has spread. A thank you note from him, an artfully designed handicraft, is one of my prized momentos. He can appear on my show any time he wishes, only I won't be there!

"A kiss on the lips is quite sentimental, but diamonds are a girl's best friend." Carol Channing visited the "Good Morning Show" following her starring role in the Broadway musical. I can still hear the raspy echo of her distinctive voice. It reminds me of NASCAR 43's exhaust, the racer driven during most of the "Good Morning Show" years by King Richard Petty of Level Cross. Richard lives just down the road from the "Good Morning Show" studio, but we didn't get together until November, 1979.

The series of interviews I taped with the legendary racer included his wife Lynda. I walked away from that interview with a lasting impression of Lynda's enormous courage, proof positive that behind Richard's determina-tion to succeed was an equally committed wife and mother. When I looked into her eyes I saw years of happy and heartbreaking moments, and endless days and nights at race tracks across the NASCAR circuit. I looked at Richard's overwhelming collection of trophies and memorabilia and marveled at the tangible metallic evidence of phenomenal success. But what I really came to admire about Richard is the unique sense of presence he radiates. When you're with Richard you are with a man who is larger than life.

I talked with the Pettys again in 1995 shortly after the King's retirement. I found him rocking away in his Carolina room at ease, cowboy hat and dark glasses in place, the calmer image of a racing legend. Later we chatted about racing and retirement and politics and children. It was the kind of conversation we can have out in the country, trading the anecdotes that bind us. It wasn't an interview, it was talking to friends you had known all your life, in the spotlight one minute, sitting and rocking the next. We bantered about some of the old dirt tracks, dust and mud clods at places like Lancaster,

S.C., and figured out that life and success was something you made out of commitment, hard work and occasionally tears.

Sometimes, I just have to stop and remind myself that a little insecure kid who grew up in Concord, almost too bashful to speak to any- one, had during the course of his career encountered and conversed with some of the world's most exceptional people. Interviewing has never been a passive experience. I am always seeking, probing for the key, the ingredient that distinguishes a celebrity from the rest of us, hoping that my interview will convey to a child or an adult some treasure that will inspire and change a life.

Viewers ask, do you ever get nervous when you're interviewing celebrities? Let me say it this way: Interviewing is a learned art. As a neophyte radio and TV broadcaster I was often overwhelmed in the presence of celebrities. You might say frozen! After all I was a teenager when I interviewed my first celebrity on WABZ in 1949. The honoree was Charlie Spivak, sideman for a number of Big Bands including the Tommy Dorsey Orchestra, and di-

rector of his own orchestra. I did okay but I bathed myself in sweat.

B-Western hero Lash LaRue was the second celebrity and the first movie star I interviewed. Our gabfest went a little better because we discussed the intricacies of handling the whip that was LaRue's trademark. Anybody can be a great interviewer if they do their homework on the interviewee, ask general questions to open up certain topics, and listen to answers that prompt more specific questions.

Sometimes an interview builds a sense of trust and respect between the two parties. Take Billy "Crash" Craddock for example. I interviewed "Crash" when he was hanging sheetrock and singing at Fred Koury's Plantation Supper Club. I watched him struggle to make it in Nashville, shared the excitement when he recorded his first hit, caught snatches of his career successes and helped promote one of his benefits. Occasionally we'd run into each other at the local "fish house."

Then, out of the blue, I was invited to share the big party his fans tossed for him on his 25th anniversary in show business. I listened to two and a half hours of accolades for "Crash," remembering his first appearances on TV as a kid, his battle to succeed and feeling proud just to have known him. That evening Anne and I shared a life we had seen blossom and grow and it was like a good old-fashioned church meeting. And on the dais there was "Crash" with that presence, a vitality tempered with assurance, poise and confidence. That is what an authentic celebrity is all about.

Experiencing celebrity is sharing a studio with Charles Kuralt and Bob Timberlake. They brought this huge book project to the studio for their interview. Their collaboration cost more than I made in a month and Kuralt's prose read like petals you'd decorate a monument with; I remember wanting to shut my eyes and listen to him rumble in that rumpled suit he wore that seemed to embody a prosaic machine. And then Timberlake chimed in with that soft, mesmerising voice that literally brushes words inside your ear. I stand in awe of artistic giants; in their presences you feel evidences of the gifts they have nurtured, of the icons they have made of themselves and yet

they are humble, self-deprecating men and women. And perhaps that is the lesson they teach; success is not riches, it is a whisper one hears inside when the Master says well done.

But there was one celebrity who literally scared me to death, a man who knew more about guns than any man in the world, a man convicted of second-degree murder who invented the M-1 Carbine, one of World War II's major infantry weapons. David Marshall "Carbine" Williams' story was first told in the MGM movie "Carbine Williams" [1952] starring Jimmy Stewart as Williams, with Jean Hagan as his wife Maggie. I interviewed Carbine at his home near Godwin in the mid '60s.

Williams had mellowed by then but he still wore a .45 on his hip and seldom smiled. There was an arsenal of handcrafted weapons in his shop and a case of dynamite under the steps set to blow up anybody who threatened to steal his guns. During the interview Carbine showed me how to fire his prototype .22 caliber machine gun designed to rattle off 2,000 bullets a minute. Cameraman John Page rolled his film as Carbine seated the ammunition belt. Stupidly, I had the trigger depressed and when Carbine slammed the bolt down a wave of slugs cascaded across a nearby cornfield. I was so shocked I couldn't release the trigger.

Page collapsed with laughter and Carbine stomped around in a circle cursing and calling me every name in the book. Hey, I was a veteran. I had fired machine guns, but never a homemade model. I really thought Carbine was going to shoot me when he looked me dead in the eye and said, "What do you think you are, some kind of a G...D..machine gun expert?" I apologized and Carbine relented. Later, when we had finished the interview we shot skeet and made up. When we drove away from the farm Carbine watched after us from the middle of the sand-furrowed road. The .45 was holstered on his hip and there were tears in his eyes.

Maria Beale Fletcher, North Carolina's first Miss America.

Sebastian Cabot, a jolly ebullient man for all seasons.

Shepherd Strudwick, Hollywood star character actor, was one of the "GMS's" first guests.

Carol Channing, hilariously entertaining and at home on WFMY's set.

Jeanne Swanner, Miss North Carolina 1964.

Actor John Forsythe visited the "Good Morning Show."

Jayne Mansfield with family, husband Mickey Hargitay and son, Zoltan.

Heart-throb Bob Conrad excited many women with his appearance on WFMY.

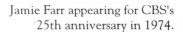

Jamie Farr appearing for CBS's 25th anniversary in 1974.

Chatting with Will Geer was like visiting with a member of the family.

Mike Connors shared his experiences
with stardom and show-business.

Actors Ed Asner and Cloris Leachman
entertained viewers during their visit.

Lee interviews Leonard Nimoy before he
became Dr. Spock.

Carbine Williams designed one of the world's great weapons, the M-1 Carbine.

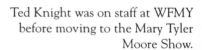

Starlet Mamie Van Doren appeared on the "Good Morning Show."

Ted Knight was on staff at WFMY before moving to the Mary Tyler Moore Show.

SIX

The Only Way to Go is First Class

Jay Wilkinson

Lee inside Kremlin in front of cathedral. 1986

"Ladies and Gentlemen, this is your Captain speaking. If you will glance out the portside of the aircraft you can see the lights of the eastern seaboard from Baltimore to the tip of Maine. We've got ourselves a beautiful night to skirt the Atlantic coast before turning east off Halifax. Just ahead is New York and on beyond is Boston. If there's anything we can do to make you more comfortable please let us know. I'll talk with you again after we leave Nova Scotia and give you further details about the rest of our flight to London Heathrow. Enjoy your evening."

In January, 1981, Pan American Airways still ruled the gravitational universe with their soaring fleet of romantic Boeing 747 clippers. On this particular evening "Good Morning Show" Director Jay Wilkinson, cameraman Gary Whiting and I were relaxing in our first-class recliners flying from Dulles International Airport near Washington to London. As I settled deeper into the supple leather cradle I recalled the day and the hour when I decided to seriously pursue the production of a series of international travel features for the "Good Morning Show."

In January, 1978, while on assignment in Washington we passed Dulles as the wheels of a 747 Clipper touched the runway. "Boys," I bragged, "our next videotaping junket will be on one of those babies." Back in Greensboro I called Merle Richman, a PR representative for Pan Am who had introduced the 747 on "The Good Morning Show" in the early '70s.

"Merle, remember when you told me that if I ever wanted to take a crew anywhere in the world all I had to do was call you?"

"Where do you want to go?"

"Holland."

"When?"

That had been three years ago and here we were again flitting through the star-filled evening toward Europe. A flight attendant momentarily interrupted my reverie. I selected several samples of caviar-laced munchies and studied my surroundings. I was in seat number one, Wilkinson in two and Whiting across the aisle in three, the front row in first class. We had all the leg room in the world in loungers that reclined to comfortable sleeping positions.

In the nose of the 747 below the flight deck the first class cabin's atmosphere was that of an exclusive club. Brandy, newspapers, flowers, and hors-d'ouveres graced a small serving table at the center rear of the cabin. Guests were encouraged to help themselves. While one flight attendant bestowed orange juice and champagne, another presented the first class gift, an elaborately packaged overnight toilet kit, including a pair of warm socks to replace our shoes, headsets for the movie and stereo entertainment and a mask for the eyes should one wish to sleep while the movie spun the night away between Washington and London.

Our cabin mates were suave, tailored gentlemen and svelte, fragrant women in exquisite designer fashions, silk, leather and real suede. Secure in our navy blue polyester blazers we affected the same sophistication as the paying passengers. They paid big bucks to get here. We were riding gratis. They belonged and we didn't, but our evils were hidden. None of our fellow passengers knew we wore frayed jockey shorts, or that the tops of our socks were slumped around our ankles. I savored the aroma of wealth, power, adventure and vintage champagne.

"Sir?" The purser was at my elbow presenting the dinner menu and eliciting reservations for dining in the upper cabin, that marvelous bubble behind the flight deck on the 747's upper fuselage. The cover of the menu was suitable for framing, a Dong Kingman watercolor of London's House of Parliament with Big Ben prominently beckoning the "Good Morning Show" crew to the banks of the Thames. I selected to dine at 10 p.m.

About the cabin, Glenfidditch and Wild Turkey were poured from real bottles, no travel-trash miniatures in this elegant drawing room! There were iced vodka and chilly accents, clipped, precise, a barbecued Texas drawl, a throaty laugh muffled by a diamond choker. There were no laptops then, no pocket calculators; a few of the men slipped out old-fashioned legal pads sheathed in rich leather briefcases, or selected prestigious newspapers from yet another solicitous flight attendant. We scanned with reverent countenances the op-ed pages of the *New York Times* and *The Washington Post* as if we understood what their journalists were carping about.

Toying with the Hors d'Oeuvre Gastronomiques I approached the most difficult decision of the evening. Should I select the Roti Au Vol, Veau a la Creme, Supreme de Volaille Chasseur, Turbot Americaine or Plat de Jour? What the heck was all this stuff anyway and just for a moment I wondered what Anne and the kids were having for dinner tonight while Pop flew the Atlantic.

I'm not implying that Lee Kinard's TV crew bankrupted Pan American World Airways, but we flew first-class on numerous flights until airline deregulation drastically downgraded our lifestyle. Our benefactor Merle Richman was downsized into retirement and we were relegated to the rear of numerous, less elegant airlines.

International travel is a living dream out of my childhood fantasies. The wonderment of the world was inspired by authors like Mary Mapes Dodge and broadcasters like Ed Murrow and the global explorer Lowell Thomas. I discovered the world through the radio when the Germans marched into Poland on September 1, 1939. From that moment World War II dominated my childhood and adolescence.

What I heard about on the radio as a child I longed to see as an adult and the "Good Morning Show" helped make this dream come true. My travels have taken me across the face of a Europe I knew only from Pathe Newsreels and *Life Magazine*. They have transported me to meet kids my own age who survived the London Blitz and others who endured Allied firebombing in the basements of Dresden.

Why I selected the Netherlands for the first travelog in 1978 is an interesting story I use to promote the magic of reading. One of my favorite childhood books was *Hans Brinker and the Silver Skates* by Mary Mapes Dodge. I was thoroughly captivated by her tale of the little Dutch boy who plugged a leaking dyke with his finger to save his village from flooding. Forty years later the spirit of "The Hero of Harlem" inspired the "Good Morning Show's" inaugural international junket to Holland.

Hook up your seatbelt and let me share some of our memorable adventures. First a word about my crew. By now I hope you've figured out that the "we" I continually refer to means "me and my crew." When we began traveling in the late '70s we needed a crew of four just to manage and maintain our gear. Since video camera, audio and recorder are now a single unit the crew is me and a videojournalist. These men are the soul and sinew of the "Good Morning Show" travel series. There haven't been many, but they have all been college graduates, aesthetically inclined, culturally aware, exceptionally creative and strong as oxen. Nothing Lee Kinard asks them to do is easy: hang out the doors of helicopters, climb high mountains, towers, temples and trees, fly around the world and go to

work immediately upon landing, stay up all night mending gear, shoot two plus hours of video every day with one eye shut while carrying nearly 50 pounds of camera gear.

It was a blustery day on the precipitous northern coast of Ireland. When we finished videotaping the sea slashing into the rocks hundreds of feet below Fairhead I volunteered to carry the camera back down the precarious slope. I knew any one of us could slip in the mire, drop the camera and put us out of business at a crucial point in the trip. I figured that since I was the leader of the band I was the more cautious. If the camera were dropped I wanted to be the one dropping it. Then I could only blame myself.

Mind you now sheep had grazed on this boggy mound for at least two millennia, the soft rich sod reeking with their memories, some so recent as to be identifiably frosted to the thick grass on a bitterly cold afternoon. I began descending the treacherous soggy incline, side-stepping to keep my footing, balancing the camera across my chest with both arms when the inevitable happened. As my feet began to slip from beneath me I cradled the camera closer as my body settled sublimely into slime and weed. Neither heel could stem the fatal slide through pools of oily goo. I felt the dampness on my backside soaking sports jacket, shirt, underwear. The useless London Fog raincoat strung out behind me like the flairing wings of a fluttering bat. Now I slewed around and the mud came toward the camera like an avalanche as a trio of laughs pealed across the bog, the sky broke away from the clouds and the sun laughed a wind that chilled my muddy carcass to the bone.

Luckily, we were traveling with our personal gear that miserable day. While my bemused colleagues snickered in the van I changed behind an outbuilding. The park at Fairhead was closed for the season. That was good for the naked man behind the shed, but what, I wondered, will they think in the spring when they will find a discarded v-neck Tee, a pair of Jockey shorts, and Burlington Gold Toes blackened with mire and stamped "Made in the U.S.A."?

In August, 1945, I screamed with joy when my radio bulletined the dropping of an atomic device on Hiroshima, Japan. "Kill the Japs," I shouted in joy, believing this strange new weapon would bring my father home from Admiral Halsey's Third Fleet. Then in 1988 the other side of the story seized me when I walked through the Peace Park in Hiroshima. Thousands of Japanese middle school children were incinerated that morning, children my age in whose deaths I had rejoiced. Entrapped by the artifacts of their holocaust I wondered why is it that a kid in Concord, N.C., no better than any other kid in the world, gets to enjoy a full life while thousands of children in another part of the world are vaporized in an instant. For me it was no longer a question of the bomb's use, but of fate and time and place and power.

On New Zealand's South Island we spent the night in a remote lodge beneath Mt. Cook, the spectacular 12,349-foot peak where Sir Edmund Hillary, the conqueror of Mt. Everest, had practiced climbing. It was still black when I awakened to the sound of birds cawing and cackling beyond the French doors that opened onto a balcony. From this platform we would, depending on the weather, videotape the sunrise glistening on the ragged ice-capped spear-like peak. A few minutes later cameraman David Plotkin and I huddled in the dawn chilled by a glacial mist burrowing into our sweaters.

We remembered previous sunrises recorded from Norwegian fjords and Thai temples. We recollected driving down the southeast coast of England from Canterbury to Rye, a black frost glazing the macadam, making the driving risky and then melting near the

Lee visiting Stonehenge in 1981.

White Cliffs of Dover. Just west of Ireland I raised the shade on the British Caledonian DC-10 and counted seven jets stacked beyond and above us, contrailing the heavens over the British Isles. In any part of the world the sunrise had always been the best part of the day for me and the lost part of my life. I had driven to the "Good Morning Show" through most of my life-allotted dawns, bringing them to fruition for others with the weather, sports and news.

When the first orange rays ignited the icy slash of Mt. Cook's peak the shrill cries of the blackbirds crescendoed and evaporated between the jagged crags. Below our camera the lodge guests walked out into the dawn "ooing and ahhing," filling the air with their cries as the birds had done in the last shadows of the night and then they, like the dawn's feathered audience, were silenced by the sheer splendor of it all and perched gaping.

The Chinese! What a strange, contradictory people. In Beijing I asked my affable guide to arrange a videotaping of Tianamen Square, the immense plaza housing the government and the tomb of Mao Zedong. When I learned the fee was $1,500 I decided to videotape it from the van as we drove its angles. That is how we purloined Tianamen Square, the scene of a dreadful massacre a year and a half later.

I expected an even higher fee for videotaping the Great Wall of China, but an afternoon there cost only $15. The Wall is so stunning to the consciousness that if the wind had not been sandblasting me in gusts to 40 miles an hour, I would have pinched myself to realize that I was really seeing this wonder of the world and not merely imagining it. As opposed to one single Wall it darted off in all directions, tenacle-like, lofty, excruciating angles that wore away my leg and thigh muscles and turned my chest into a bellows. By the time we finished videotaping a dust storm had driven all the tourists from its heights, so David Plotkin videotaped a classic shot of me walking alone down the Great Wall of China.

Videotaping fees are a thorn in my budget so we have devised extreme measures to obtain expensive shots for

Lee petting an Australian outback wallaby.

free, including the interior of the Coliseum in Rome. We recorded the Sphinx from a hole in the wall of an Egyptian garbage dump, but I was willing to pay $50 to videotape the tomb of King Tut. In Australia we were almost jailed for videoing a naked Prime Minister. This bizarre experience began when I hired a helicopter to use as a platform for aerial shots of the Sydney area. We removed a door to provide cameraman David Plotkin maneuvering room for videotaping from our designated 1,500-foot altitude. The pilot warned that the winds were gusty and that he would do his best to hold the craft steady. For some long minutes we hovered just beyond the Sydney Tower to get some magnificent cover shots of the city.

I found out we were under investigation by the Australian version of the FBI when agents knocked on my hotel door demanding to screen our raw aerial footage. Our pilot was in deep trouble. All that hovering over Sydney occurred above the home of the Australian Prime Minister, who according to the cops "just happened to be bathing in the buff with his lady."

The investigator continued; "You know we saw an object [like a gun] protruding from the chopper and could have shot you down."

"Are you serious," I asked incredulously.

"Dead serious," was his curt reply.

"So, what are you going to do, arrest us?"

Turned out he wasn't interested in taking us in, he just wanted to screen our videotape to make certain we were who we represented ourselves to be and that we had not videoed the Prime Minister in the "buff."

In 20 years of globe-circling we have enjoyed precious few encounters with cops. In 1979 we drove from Dublin to war-scarred Belfast, Northern Ireland. We were videotaping background material for a series on the Irish Children's Summer Program. This project invited Catholic and Protestant children from Belfast's sectarian segregated housing projects to Greensboro where they could learn to know each other in a friendly setting.

One of the early supporters of the program administered by Agnes Hughes was Greensboro clinical psychologist John Edwards. Belfast was an armed camp, barricaded and deserted on a Saturday night. Rubbernecking like a tourist, John missed a red light and in a split second we were surrounded by a squad of armored cars.

An officer approached Edwards' window. "Good evening, sir. Do you realize that you have run a red light?"

Shaken by the show of military force, John apologized in a quavering eastern Carolina drawl, "I'm sorry, sir. This is the first time I have ever driven into Belfast and I'm lost. I was so busy looking for the right road I didn't see the red light."

After a momentary pause the entire detachment broke into convulsive laughter. They were highly amused at Edwards' southern drawl and replayed the joke among themselves in their unintelligible brogue. After exchanging a few pleasantries, the officer directed us to our hotel—which I will always remember for the sign in the bathroom offering directions for our escape should the IRA bomb the establishment.

All of my trips to Northern Ireland have been memorable. At dusk in Ballycastle we checked into a hotel honeycombed with coffin-sized rooms and cots. The lodge was being remodeled so the rates were right but the rooms were cold. We survived on body heat in the "spit and sawdust" pub, but going to bed was an Arctic nightmare. I undressed quickly and pulling on my flannel pajamas slid under a mountain of quilts and then shock! My feet sank into a warm, mushy mass.

I sat straight up as male screams echoed simultaneously along the hall. Our gracious hosts had placed hot water bottles at the foot of our beds to warm our feet, but my colleagues had never experienced the erotic thrill of sinking toes into these rubbery heaters and were fearfully jolted. We could have enjoyed a fine night's sleep had not one of our group delighted himself too long at the Bushmill's Distillery barrel and spent the night praying for salvation at the rim of the fraternal toilet.

Travel teaches that you can get into a lot of trouble in an international restroom. In September, 1979, Larry Fitzgerald, John Edwards and I were zipping down the autobahn from Frankfurt to Lucerne, Switzerland, when we opted for a rest stop. I selected a stall and locked the door. Finishing their business, Fitzgerald and Edwards went back to the van. I reached for the stall's door handle and pulled it. It wouldn't open. I tried again, and again. This is foolish, I thought. Surely, there is no way this door could be locked. Ever so slowly and methodically I placed my hand on the knob turned it slowly and pulled. Nothing! Panic attack!

I was trapped in a lavatory stall in a roadside rest stop on the autobahn. Visions of Hitler's gas chambers drowned my courage. Flustered, I looked for a way under or over the door. There was no escape. I yelled for five minutes. No answer. Silence. I thought I was losing my mind. I must be calm, I told myself as I reached for the doorhandle one more time and pulled. It wouldn't open. Angrily, I pushed at the door and fell headlong from the stall onto the floor. The door opened outward instead of inward. I walked back to the van elated, thrilled to be free again. Edwards gave me a strange look when I settled onto the seat beside him.

"We thought we'd lost you," he said quizzically.

"Yes," I replied fully knowing what real relief was all about. "I had the same feeling."

In Florence, Italy, I was standing in the tub showering with one of those flexible shower heads Europeans favor when I inadvertently sprayed the ceiling light bulb. It exploded in a shower of sparks leaving me in the dark threatened by fragments of glass about the floor and in the water. "Good Morning Show" producer Jack Hilliard and I were rooming together. "Jack," I screamed. "Help me. Open the bathroom door." No answer. I had two choices: electrocution, or slashing my feet on broken glass. I opted to waste my feet. Gingerly, I eased out of the tub which set on a precarious ledge and felt about the floor with my toes for glass. Finding none I stretched for the door knob and escaped. Totally impervious to my misfortune, Jack lay fast asleep.

In Russia one rule to follow is "NEVER drink the water." Stay with bottled water or bottled beverages and never put ice in your glass. They have a form of "epizutis" that will disable you in minutes. Our crew was so sick for two weeks that Ylena (Helen), our somewhat arrogant KGB guide, observed, "The toilet must be you Americans' favorite room in the house for that's where you spend all your time."

Most of my guides have been diligent, intelligent, committed to their country and pleasant. Ylena vacillated

Lee with kilt-clad Scottishman.

between kindness and arrogance leading to a stormy relationship between a card-carrying member of the Communist party and a good old fashioned patriotic American boy. We were standing on the cliffs above Yalta looking out across the expanse of the Black Sea, eating watermelon the old fashioned way—without utensils.

"Do you have watermelon in America?" Ylena inquired.

"Oh yes, it's a great favorite in the South. Did your spies steal it like they did the secrets for the atom bomb?"

"Lee," this time a purring superior voice. "I bet your satellite is watching you right now. I understand it can read writing on a sheet of paper."

At this point Gorbachev's glasnost was a tentative, debatable idea. I answered firmly. "You're right Helen. You don't think for one minute I would come over here and put myself at the mercy of you people without knowing that if I got in trouble, I could hold up a sign saying H-E-L-P and my people would come and get me!"

After dinner on our final night in St. Petersburg, Helen announced she was going to the train station to purchase our tickets to Moscow.

"Please get first-class tickets, Helen. I'll pay for them if I have to."

"Lee, trains in the Soviet Union have no first-class."

That is an understatement. The train we rode was built for a truly class-less society. Shortly after midnight we lugged six equipment boxes and three personal suitcases into a wooden cell on the train. For security reasons the trains between St. Petersburg and Moscow ran only at night. Go figure! They hauled mobile missiles ready for launching back and forth between the two cities.

There were four bunks. One for each member of the crew and yes, one for Helen. We stowed the gear in the middle of the floor between the bunks and sat glumly, prisoners in our own little gulag. I went to bed quickly in one of the top bunks as far away from Ylena as I could get. When I woke up about seven I looked down to see where Ylena spent the night. Engineer Bob King was sitting on the side of his bunk practicing misery.

"Hey Bob. Where's Ylena?"

"You were snoring so loudly she got up and left about a half-hour ago."

When I elaborate on this story in talks about "Good Morning Show" travels the punch line is, "Helen is the only woman other than my wife I ever slept with!"

Inevitably Ylena got even. She withheld the traveler's checks I had presumably lost in Yalta until the evening we departed for the States, then smirked when Aeroflot's bandits parched my bankroll for $2,400 for baggage overweight after permitting me to fly the TV gear free from Washington to Moscow.

Viewers ask, "Does your wife travel with you?" Not as a rule, but she has enjoyed all the "Good Morning Show" anniversary trips with fans. Together we have enjoyed beautiful moments in Holland, Scandinavia, France, Germany, Austria, Switzerland, England and Scotland. I will always remember the snowy day at Giverny we videotaped in Monet's Garden, the Saturday we visited Edvard Grieg's yellow and green cottage above Bergen, and the day we interviewed Thor Heyerdahl in Oslo's Viking Ship museum. Anne and I saw the D-Day Beaches of Normandy for the first time and watched Paris preparing for the Bicentennial of the French Revolution in 1989.

Are there some special moments from 20 years of travel that I treasure? Watching birds fly through a huge yellow full moon on the Nile at Luxor, seeing the pyramids at Giza, studying Australia's Blue Mountains from a rocky ledge, contemplating Stonehenge, gazing down on Tintern Abbey in the footsteps of Wordsworth, and living next to his Dove Cottage in the Lake District, chasing the monster across the black expanse of Lochness, marching with a bagpiper in the Scottish Highlands, sampling champagne with the Krug brothers in their caves at Rheims, watching the sun rise on the Temple of the Dawn by the Chao Praya in Bangkok, seeing the eclipse from the New Zealand Alps in April 1986, sailing out of Helsinki and into Stockholm through their respective archipelagoes, watching the changing of the guard at Lenin's Tomb in Red Square from my room in the National Hotel, picking pebbles from Omaha Beach and crying in the cemetery above the bloodied strand, feeling faint on the angular ledge of the Leaning Tower of Pisa and imagining Juliet on her balcony in Verona.

The "Good Morning Show" travelogs were designed to provide the program with a different "look" and to improve its ratings. Viewers thank me for taking them places they say they could never go. But the biggest joy the travelogs bring to me is the opportunity to show them in classrooms across the Piedmont. Hopefully, the vignettes have provided a comparative look at some of the world's major cultures. Perhaps one day these students will have the inspiration and opportunity to travel and broaden their personal horizons.

The segments were intentionally produced to educate rather than entertain. I offered my viewers the opportunity to discover the world through my eyes. While some segments were anecdotal most dealt seriously with art, history, archaeology, music, science, crafts, whatever I found significantly intriguing about the culture of a country. I have walked in the European footsteps of my Celtic forebears, watched the fairy penguins come ashore on Australia's Phillip Island. I have chatted with koalas playing through the gum trees near Melbourne. I have pumped ale and debated politics in a Canterbury pub, savored stump water with Gideon in the Scottish highlands. In St. Petersburg I saw what Peter the Great built and Elizabeth II bought. It took half a lifetime, but I made those old ESSO travelogs I watched as a kid at Clara Harris School in the late '30s come to life on videotape.

I will end this chapter with two unusual adventures loosely related and involving beautiful women. The first had its beginning in Pinehurst where I interviewed Thailand's Queen Sirikit and was invited to lunch. We dined in early 1981 while she was visiting her paratrooper son at Ft. Bragg. This exceptionally gorgeous woman was dedicated to promoting the arts and crafts of Thailand's mountain tribes, hoping to turn them from the opium trade.

In the most regal setting you can imagine, with ladies-in-waiting scurrying on hands and knees across the floor in all directions, the Queen ordered fried chicken and french fries with Coke for our lunch. Her secretary, an equally delightful woman joined us though the Queen, who had been educated in France, did not need an interpreter. We talked about the "Good Morning Show" travel itinerary and the fact that we had not visited Thailand. I left the table with a Royal invitation to visit the country and a few months later four of us winged halfway around the world to Bangkok, which just has to be the world's most exotic city.

Our first evening in Bangkok we were invited to an audience with Queen Sirikit. At the hotel we grabbed a few hours sleep and began videotaping in 100-degree-plus temperatures. On location in 110-plus heat we changed from sweat-soaked work clothes into suits and ties and arrived for the audience with every stitch of clothing clinging to us like seaweed. Graciously ignoring our disheveled appearance the Queen's secretary inquired about our choice of refreshments. Four men hung their sweating faces in misery and gloom. I knew what was on their minds, bourbon and ginger, Scotch Malt, cold beer. I finally broke the silence, "Ma'am, we would love to have some ice cold beer, if you have some in the fridge!" We were quite refreshed when summoned to the Queen's chamber.

Our most preposterous travel experience began en route to Bangkok in the transit bar at Hong Kong Airport. While our flight was being refueled, our travelog quartet scanned the duty free shops and relaxed at the bar. It must have been four in the morning when "the girl" sauntered up to the counter with a guy. She surely was wearing what she had been born in, white jeans, a mauve blouse, black hair. You knew if you took your eyes away you'd never again see anything so erotically curvaceous in your life.

She was towing a gigolo drifter, long unkempt curls, loose-fitting, white hopsack jeans and shirt, the type you see in deodorant ads, probably a soccer-stud. We whiled the time away until our flight was called speculating on where she was from and where she was going, then back to the clipper. I dozed. After all, we had been flying from Greensboro to Bangkok through New York, Tokyo and Hong Kong for what seemed like a couple of days. I was portside in first class, second row on the aisle. Mark was beside me in the window seat fast asleep. Terry was opposite me across the aisle in the first row with Jay snoozing beside him in the window seat.

For some reason I opened my eyes just as "the girl" brushed by me and made a right turn to stop directly in front of Terry. She touched him on the shoulder as she popped the top button on her jeans. As he raised his head and opened his eyes she slid her jeans down across her hips. Ceremoniously they accordioned at her ankles. Her body was like bone china in a brilliant light. From where I sat the blue veins beneath her translucent skin were illuminated by the somber glow of the sleepy cabin.

She whispered in Terry's ear. McMahon shook his head. The girl reached down and pulled her jeans up ever so slowly. At that moment I knew we were going to die. Her gigolo must be poised to burst into the cabin. There would be some kind of a scene and it would turn violent. It had to be a setup of some kind. A girl just doesn't walk into first class and hit on a guy in the midst of his buddies. To this day I don't know what she saw in McMahon. Under intense questioning, McMahon said he didn't understand a thing the girl said. He had failed his first test in universal language.

Three days later we were videotaping a folk arts performance near Bangkok. A man and a woman set up a still camera near us and began photographing the same dance routine. Sure enough it was Miss Mile High and her consort. Mark Conrad tapped her on the shoulder and said, "Pardon me, Miss. Haven't we SEEN you somewhere before?"

Since April, 1978, "Good Morning Show" hosts have made nearly 50 trips abroad to produce travel segments, primarily for the November and May sweeps. We have visited the British Isles, Scandinavia, the USSR, Japan, The People's Republic of China, Australia, New Zealand, all of Western Europe, East Germany after The Wall, the Czech Republic, Hungary, Greece, Hawaii plus eastern and western Canada. While it's true that I have logged the vast majority of the junkets, co-hosts Kim Skeen, Tracy Wilson and Doug Allred have also had their passports validated in distant lands.

Viewers ask, who does your research? I do my own! My life is a preparation for what I produce for TV. A single travel series of 15- to 24-minute segments is in research and production for approximately four months.

Lee Kinard's Top Ten Places in the World:

1. Provence
2. Nice
3. Wales
4. England
5. Mt. Cook, New Zealand
6. London
7. Paris
8. Stockholm
9. Scotland
10. Bavaria

Lee Kinard's most enjoyable trip:
Provence, France, September 1995.

SEVEN

Writers and Books

Lee interviewing Greensboro author Dave Morrah in 1964.

Reading and writing is at the foundation of my life, and books and authors form a pillar of the "Good Morning Show." They represent content, creativity, inspiration, knowledge and experience. In this parcel I'll recall my infatuation with reading and writing. I'll tell you about the authors I've interviewed in the studio and in the field, and on exotic locations ranging from Oslo, Norway, to Devon, England. I'll tell you about the television features they inspired and how these encounters enriched my life, my program and hopefully the lives of my audience.

My love affair with books began where my most perfectible dreams were born, in the presence of my grandmothers and my mother. You could find me in Mom Winecoff's kitchen on any liberated Saturday, or summer days, hanging on her coattails. As a hovering oldest grandchild listening was what I did best, a kid enthralled by spider-webbed plots of ancient Carolina themes, marriages, births, deaths and the foremost tragedy, The War Between the States. That's where I learned that only the damned Yankees called it The Civil War and that William Tecumseh Sherman was the son of Satan.

When Mom Winecoff described Reconstruction I saw her stories as in a movie, sepia-tinted frames of her father struggling home barefooted from his Civil War POW camp. He was a walking stick figure half-hidden in the young summer haze when she first caught a glimpse of him coming down the road near Ramah Church. There was my great-grandfather Corporal Robert Lawson Hill, way off yonder and coming on, seeking out his home across the fallow folds of broom-sage Piedmont fields. Home, he found his dream still-born for lack of seed and mule and plow and sunup-to-sundown gee-hawing and whoa-boying.

"They took Daddy prisoner," Mom said, pulling the broom straw out of the pound cake, measuring it against a lonesome ray of sunlight; clean as a whistle it was; the spirit of the cake was pure with "nary a sad streak," which was pretty doggone important. As I ate the moon-pie-size sample baked specially for me in a small tin, I thought about the old soldier choking on dust and vinegar, dodging the flesh-and-bone-shattering minie balls and grape shot. I wondered how many Yankees he killed, if any at all. If he had only written it down I would have owned bragging rights for a hundred adolescent bull sessions. But all he recorded was where he camped. There were huge gaps in the diary my imagination laced with fantasies.

My infatuation with the Civil War and the volumes that told its history was further fueled by numerous trips to Charleston, S.C., to visit Grandmother Kinard. Charleston in the late 1930s was suffering at the height of The Great Depression. Too many of the stately antebellum homes in the Peninsula Historic District had been reduced to rooming houses or havens for vagrants.

Just after dawn Mother and I would walk the cobbled streets gawking at the hucksters who pushed their carts of fruits and vegetables through the lanes singing out their wares through the baking humidity. From Battery Park we looked across the harbor to Ft. Sumter. Here the first shots launched The War Between the States. For the first time I heard history's fated names, Beauregard, Lee, Lincoln and Davis. By the time I celebrated my 12th birthday I had read every book on the War Between the States in the Concord Public Library, setting the foundation for a whole series of "Good Morning Show" features in the 1960s.

Eccentricities defined Grandmother Kinard. I never knew her really well, or perhaps at all. She was said to have suffered from the vapors, leading me to believe that she may have been a model for a younger Scarlet O'Hara. She thrived on BC Headache Powders and seldom donned a dress, preferring to languish through the day in a nightgown and housecoat. She was thin as a rail, her skin was delicate parchment. She spoke in a whispery voice, softly, gently, seeming always to belong somewhere else.

She only gave me one present in my entire life. It was a defining moment. Let me describe the time and place. It was a typical Charleston summer evening, the air rich with humidity-soaked oleander and as still as a brick. The sun had just given up Charleston but Grandmother lay propped on pillows in her bed. I sat on the edge as we talked and then glancing toward her open closet noticed a tall stack of paper stashed in the far corner.

"What is that Grandma, that stack of paper in the closet?"

"That's a book I'm writing, Sonny."

"What's it about?"

"People I have known in Charleston."

Considering all the fuss I had heard about "Gone With the Wind" I was impressed. Imagine my grandmother writing a book.

That was the last time I saw Grandmother Kinard. As far as I know nothing ever became of that manuscript in the closet. But that moment generated a life-long interest in writers; what did creating stories that would make a stack of paper that high involve? When we were struggling to find content for the program it occurred to me that interviewing authors and doing book reviews was a great way to meet creative celebrities and fill time.

My first author interview actually took place on WABZ Radio in Albemarle. The celebrity was Fred Ross of Badin, author of *Jackson Mahaffey*, winner of the 1951 Houghton Mifflin Literary Fellowship Award. One of the first authors I welcomed to the "Good Morning Show" was Burke Davis who introduced *Our Incredible Civil War* to our audience in 1960. Davis published more than 50 books including biography, fiction and children's stories. His biographies of Stonewall Jackson, Robert E. Lee and Jeb Stuart are eminently popular in reprints and expensive in first editions. Burke's strong suit was his journalistic background. He knew what research was all about and managed that function to recreate some of history's larger-than-life personalities. Davis last visited the "Good Morning Show" in 1980 to discuss *Sherman's March*.

In the early "Good Morning Show"

years one of the most popular writers in Greensboro was Dave Morrah, director of public relations and promotion at Guilford College. When we met he had been writing humorous pieces in mock German for *The Saturday Evening Post* for almost 20 years. Morrah introduced *Me and the Liberal Arts* (1962), *Der Wizzard in Ozzenland* (1962) and *Our Honor the Mayor* (1964) on the show.

I wish I had been blessed with the presence of mind in the '60s to have saved more of my author interviews, but in some cases that wasn't possible. Much of what we did was live and I wasn't prescient enough to realize that many of the authors I was interviewing and reviewing would achieve major status. I am thinking particularly of John Ehle whose "Good Morning Show" works included *Lion on the Hearth* (1961), *The Land Breakers* (1964) and *The Road* (1967).

One of the first writers whose TV interviews I did manage to save on video is Fred Chappell. I have a shelf of videotape interviews with Fred, whose work includes more than 20 books of poetry and fiction. Someday I plan to transcribe the substance of our chats. I have also had the pleasure of studying a section of English literature with Fred at the University of North Carolina at Greensboro.

Fred delivered marvelous lectures, really essays, pacing the room in front of the class, sharing his knowledge in modulated tones between those measured breaths that are his trademark, those fertile pauses that delineate an artistic control and management of language that is phenomenal. What I am struggling to describe is a mystical depth of understanding, not only of words, phrases, sentences, and meter but of tone, texture and pacing. The morning I congratulated him on winning the T. S. Eliot Award for poetry my comments on the way he "reads" elicited this explanation, which is worth its weight in verse:

"Words in poetry become personal, become part of one's experience as soon as they are absorbed in the work of art as a work of art. After that they change, they suffer a sea change as Shakespeare would say, and become part of one's own experience, not only a part of one's own experience, but also act as a catalyst to change one's experience so that you understand it, what's happened to you, how you lived in a different light and have you ever understood things before. It takes a lot of practice to do this but it's the kind of practice that's a lot of fun."

Fred writes so poignantly because his ears are super-sensitive to nuance. He separates every ripple in the stream of consciousness into its own pitch. You can experience this as I have in *Farewell, I'm Bound to Leave You* (1996).

I'd better allot the women equal time here or Doris Betts and Lee Smith will pass up the "Good Morning Show" when their next novels appear. I like these women because they are earthy! By that I mean they are women of substantial mettle, richly literary, solid, sexy, if you wish, and vigorously energetic. I like being in the presence of these women because there is something about the aura of their creativity that is invigorating. Their presence makes me feel alive! Doris Betts visited the "Good Morning Show" to introduce *The Scarlet Thread* (1964), *The River to Pickle Beach* (1972) and was mostly recently a guest in 1997 to cel-

ebrate the publication of *The Sharp Teeth of Love*. She explained how she drew various themes of an historical, mystical and contemporary nature into T*eeth* and the technique she applied to make them believable to the reader. Doris also shared her enthusiasm for the future of the novel:

"Well, I don't think the novel is at all dead and I don't think it's going to die. There are great things that film can do, video can do, but there is something that the long, written story does that you can't get any other way. Certainly in the South the novel is alive, well and thriving. Some of the women writers are the hottest in New York today. African-American writers from the South are very hot and being read world-wide and I guess the next group to come out of the South will be our Hispanic citizens because somehow it's new populations that have stories to tell that begin to emerge in America and that's very exciting."

The first Lee Smith novel I reviewed on the "Good Morning Show" was *Fancy Strut* (1973). Lee visited in 1995 to talk about *Saving Grace*. I wanted to find out how she crafted a character that fascinated me until I hung on every word. Lee had me walking around in Gracie Shepherd's mind thinking I knew this daughter of a charismatic serpent-handling itinerant preacher until she bounced away on another onery tangent. Here's how Lee described the resourceful process that evolved into *Saving Grace*:

"There are some images that I have had in my mind from when I was a child and saw this as a child and as a teenager, then later as really a student of the South who is interested in all things Southern. At this point I went back and was talking to some of these believers and became very compelled by the material. It's very, very strong material and I was sort of repelled and compelled and found the kind of conflict that needs to be present when you're writing fiction. In a certain way I'm confronting a lot of things about the South that trouble me and also that draw me. Writing this book was like being on a scary ride at a carnival, in a certain way."

Experience, conflict, tension, the melding of the creative process through time and space until interpretation spreads itself upon the pages of a novel —that process was what I was hoping to get from Lee Smith and she delivered.

My most embarrassing author interview took place on June 14, 1973 when Tom Wicker, *New York Times* columnist and Washington Bureau Chief discussed his new novel *Facing the Lions*. Since the book was about politics, that topic dominated our interview, but I erred on the stump of naivety. I suggested that surely President Nixon's overwhelming election victory in 1972 was a remarkably unifying statement about the U.S. and a huge vote of confidence in his leadership. Nixon had squashed George McGovern with 18 million popular votes while rolling up 520 Electoral College votes.

Wicker replied to the effect that, and I am paraphrasing, "A victory of that magnitude can also create a disturbing perception of power and dictatorship." A few weeks after our interview Nixon's Watergate cover-up collapsed in the struggle over the White House tapes. Wicker signed my book, "To Lee

Kinard after a good show early in the morning, June 14, 1973." I am certain that the affable Hamlet native could have sternly lectured me on the dark side of politics had he wished. Most graciously he let me off the hook with an historical perspective.

In 1975 Wicker returned to discuss *A Time to Die*. This work documented the bloody rebellion at the Attica, N.Y. Correctional Facility in 1971 that killed 33 inmates and 10 hostages.

Wilma Dykeman (Mrs. James R. Stokely, Jr.) visited the "Good Morning Show" on October the 10th, 1973, ostensibly to introduce her first novel *The Tall Woman*, a Civil War epic set in Dykeman's Great Smoky Mountains. She also brought along a reprint of *The French Broad*, a Rivers of America series classic. Dykeman wrote inspiringly about a region she knew well and in her novel about the courage of a mountain woman in a critical period of American history. The book was important for contemporary women who were beginning to seek liberation.

Bill Morris, journalist-author, introduced his first novel *Motor City* (1992) on the "Good Morning Show," and was back in 1997 to celebrate the publication of his Vietnam era novel *All Souls Day*. The Morris interview was a trip, literally. We rode to the interview in his prized 1954 Buick. The historic Buick figures prominently in Morris's life and in a provocative novel that combines historical events and personalities with fictional characters to dramatize a moment that moved the world. Much of *All Souls' Day* is set in Bangkok, a city I know well, so Bill and I chatted about that and his historical-fiction technique. At the center of *All Souls' Day* is the coup that overthrew the Ngo Dinh Diem government in 1963.

For the interview and the Buick experience Morris donned a silk suit tailored in Bangkok and slipped into a garish pair of crimson slippers sans socks. While Morris was changing into his slick suit I discovered that he writes on an old-fashioned typewriter though I think soon his success will allow him a computer upgrade—if he wants one. Morris looks the writer, lives the writer, talks the writer, is the writer. I think he'd make a terrific actor.

After interviewing Morris I came home and pulled General William

Westmoreland's book off the shelf. Westmoreland field-commanded the war from 1964 to '68 and served as Army chief of staff from 1968-72. He visited the "Good Morning Show" on February 19th, 1976. I grilled the General about the peripheral factors that manipulated America's conduct or misconduct of that war. It had taken the life of my brother-in-law and I was none too pleased with how it had been prosecuted. In *A Soldier's Report* Westmoreland points out the weight the cold war exerted on our Vietnam strategy.

Some of my most exciting interviews have occurred on foreign shores. In 1982, in the Viking Ship Museum in Oslo, Norway, I interviewed Thor Heyerdahl about his rafting adventures. The Norwegian ethnologist first won the world's headlines in 1947 when he sailed Kon Tiki, a balsa-wood raft, from Peru to the eastern Polynesian Islands. He did it to prove the islands could have been settled by South American Indians. At the time of our interview, Heyerdahl was profoundly convinced that we were killing the seas and committing suicide.

In spring, 1994, videojournalist George Vaughn and I produced a World War II D-Day series in England and France. We discovered a story that had eluded most Americans for decades. On a typical spring day in England, through gale force winds, driving rain and icy temperatures we drove to Slapton Sands on the Devon coast. We were tracking down the details behind a massive training disaster and the man who had made that tragedy public knowledge.

On the night of April 27, 1944, a rehearsal for the D-Day landings was scheduled at a secluded beach on the Devon coast. As the American transports were moving into place the landing craft were intercepted and assaulted by German torpedo boats. That night 946 American servicemen drowned at Slapton Sands. Hundreds were buried in a mass grave near the site and the disaster was hushed up.

Ken Small was the English beachcomber who had broken the story and hoisted a World War II vintage Sherman tank off the ocean floor to prove it. Driving down through the cliffs we saw the restored tank set up as a memorial in a parking lot near the beach. The only other vehicle in the car park was a small English sedan. Ken Small was sitting in the car surrounded by copies of his book, *The Forgotten Dead*, in which Small describes what he believes to be "the true story" of Slapton Sands.

It is a narrative fraught with personal trials and terrors. Unraveling the wartime mystery destroyed his marriage, bankrupted him and nearly drove him insane. Ironically, Small's adventure began when he was beachcombing after a particularly severe storm. Suddenly, before his feet a stretch of sand began to yield all kinds of military flotsam—shells, shrapnel, buttons, bits of military vehicles, and pieces of pipe. Scooping up the artifacts he couldn't help but wonder where these objects came from.

From a fisherman Small learned that an "odd object" lay off shore in sixty feet of water. The "Battle of Slapton Sands" became an obsession, but it took a decade to get the "odd object," a Sherman tank, on the beach. The interminable struggle inspired in Small a deep affection for the untrained, dis-organized American GIs who died practicing for an assault on Normandy's Utah Beach. Whatever the tank's recovery cost him Ken can't make back in the sale of books, but he can live with fond memories of the bonds forged with the American relatives of those GIs who drowned at Slapton Sands.

In the '60s I interviewed publicist-author John Harden, who wrote *The Devil's Tramping Ground and Other North Carolina Mystery Stories* (1949) and *Tarheel Ghosts* (1954). I loosely adapted some of Harden's tales for a "Good Morning Show" series and a documentary "Ghosts I have Known" for Halloween 1965. According to audience approval it may have been the most popular series I've produced. Decades later impressionable viewers still recall this crude "cut and paste" attempt to dramatize five of North Carolina's most video-adaptable ghost stories.

One book I reviewed on the "Good Morning Show" would make a great movie. In Concord I grew up hearing mysterious smatterings of adult conversation about Gaston B. Means, a young man of good means gone bad. I had forgotten this subject of clandestine gossip until 1963 when I received a copy of Edwin P. Hoyt's *Spectacular Rogue Gaston B. Means*. Hoyt's portrayal of Means characterizes Concord's most visible villain as a swindler, faker, braggart and liar, one of the most immoral thieves of the '20s and '30s.

Means' inevitable downfall was associated with one of the biggest American stories of the '30s—the Lindberg Kidnapping, "the crime of the century." Twenty-month-old Charles A. Lindberg Jr. was kidnapped from his parents' home in New Jersey on March 1, 1932. The scheming Means bilked Washington socialite Evalyn Walsh McLean of more than $100,000 as purported payment for the child's return. When Means couldn't deliver the baby J. Edgar Hoover's FBI nailed him for fraud and he went to prison.

In 1936 Bruno Richard Hauptman was executed for the murder of the Lindberg baby. On December 8, 1938, Gaston Bullock Means succumbed to a heart attack at the United States Hospital for Defective Delinquents in Springfield, Missouri. Following services at his North Union Street home, he was buried in the family plot at Concord's Oakwood Cemetery on December 15, 1938. I was seven and recall the funeral, but what intrigued me and my buddies, not to mention J. Edgar Hoover and a host of other people, was what happened to Mrs. McLean's $100,000. As children ranging Union Street in Concord we often amused ourselves hunting for Means's bounty, but just like the "Feds" we came up empty-handed.

Speaking of a far better folk hero, one of the shelves in my library is beginning to bend under the weight of Jerry Bledsoe's bountiful production. Bledsoe is an acclaimed author, but his biggest failing is that he hasn't made an honest attempt to overshadow the near-legendary Lewis Grizzard by telling his stories on stage. Evading an opportunity to be our next Will Rogers, he's opted to pursue a perilous journey to bankruptcy as a regional publisher.

Nostalgically, Bledsoe represents the greatest days of *The Greensboro Daily News*. His folksy columns brightened many a morning and still work magic in collected volumes. One of my prized Bledsoe collectibles is a signed first edition of *The World's Number One, Flat-Out, All-Time Great Stock Car Racing Book* (1975).

Bledsoe can tell a story as well as he can write it. That's why I compare him with Grizzard. Some years ago I saw possibilities for Bledsoe as a homespun philosopher on the "Good Morning Show," and spoke to our management about it. As I recall it didn't happen because the newspaper management nixed the idea.

When Jerry stretches those long legs and begins to talk I just settle back and drift with him into whatever world he is describing. I have a unique sense of pride when I see *Bitter Blood* and *Before He Wakes*, his marvelous true crime editions prominently featured in airport book stores throughout the world. Bledsoe's Christmas story *The Angel Doll* (1995) is to 20th century America what *A Christmas Carol* was to Dickens's England.

Maya Angelou is not the most accessible author even though she lives right here in the Piedmont. When we finally got together on the "Good Morn-ing Show" I quickly discovered that she is the most regally impressive woman I have met, a magnificent talent who is foremost a humanitarian. She was promoting a benefit to rebuild African-American churches burned by vandals. In that impassioned poet-philosopher's voice she delivered her plea. "My theme is that human beings are more alike than we are unlike, and if we could ever ingest that meaning, that truth, we wouldn't be so ready to throw each other to the wolves."

I began this chapter with Fred Ross's frisky tale, *Jackson Mahaffey*, and concluded with the inauguration poet Maya Angelou. I would hope that the writers' personal stories told in the interviews I have telecast might inspire viewers to discover the courage and capability to release the stories locked in their hearts. I would also hope that within the conflict of a novel, or in the simplicity of a verse they might find what all artists are continually seeking, the purest expression of truth.

EIGHT

Co-hosts: A Matter of Chemistry

"Good Morning Show" co-host Kim Skeen.

For nearly 20 years I was the "Good Morning Show's" sole host and producer. It was infinitely easier that way, a simple outline on one piece of paper, the rest in my head, winging it, making it up, having fun, performing extemporaneously and spontaneously. I didn't have to concern myself with interpersonal problems, politics, or balancing "face time" between personalities. All I had to do was television and I loved it. But TV is show business and sooner or later somebody just has to burst the bubble.

One morning the program director du jour said matter-of-factly, "You know Lee, you're getting a little age on you. You need a good looking girl sitting next to you on the 'Good Morning Show' set." At 46, I didn't have the feeling I'd aged dramatically and so I took his remarks personally. But the die was cast and I didn't fight it. I accepted what was culturally appropriate and besides I could use the help. Practically, women were hired to broaden the show's presentation of race and sex and to make it pretty.

Diana Moon: 1978-79

A strikingly beautiful first runner-up for the Miss North Carolina title, Diana Moon was the "good looking young girl" selected to co-anchor the "Good Morning Show." The Aberdeen native and Phi Beta Kappa communications major twirled onto our set straight from the Demon Deacons cheerleading squad. Diana was 22, less than half my age. The situation was not unusual for the industry, but I was uncomfortable appearing on TV with a young woman the same age as my oldest daughter.

On the brighter side I finally had a partner, if I could just bring her up to speed. The challenge was ominous. Diana had no experience anchoring, field reporting or producing. What she did have was a beautiful face and the natural ability to precisely read any piece of copy placed before her. I'm not sure Diana had worked a full day in her life and if she had it didn't involve getting up in the middle of the night to appear on TV. I watched her struggle with our ruthless schedule.

One morning as the program introduction was ending and the camera was dollying into a two shot of Diana and me at the anchor desk I glanced at her just as huge tears cascaded down her cheeks. Alarmed and embarrassed for her I signaled frantically for the camera to zoom in on me so the audience wouldn't see her crying.

Diana was miserable and exhausted and had trouble sleeping. One evening I just happened to be driving by a restaurant as Diana and her date darted out the door and down the steps at a trot. I knew he was rushing her home so she could get her rest. She would have been better off staying out until 11, grabbing a couple of hours of sleep, coming in to do the show and napping in the afternoon. Blissfully, marriage rescued Diana from the "Good Morning Show." She lives in Oklahoma City with her husband and daughter.

Suzanne Moss: 1979-80

Suzanne Moss moved from the production staff to take Moon's place. Suzanne and I had worked together on several projects before she joined the show, but we couldn't jell as a team. Our relationship on TV was short-lived, but the story has a happy ending. Moss learned the anchoring trade in Raleigh from my friend Charlie Gaddy and saw her career blossom in Richmond and Dallas.

Karen Carns: 1980-82

When Operations Manager Jack Forehand and I began searching nationwide for Moss's replacement we had our work cut out for us. TV stations across the country were expanding newscasts and sweeping up the prime talent. Early morning TV programs were not viable career choices for ambitious, attractive females. Even so we looked at more than 150 videotapes and resumes, mostly from inexperienced candidates.

In the midst of this agonizing search we screened an audition from a young woman who was hosting a noon show in Columbus, Georgia. Standing in the doorway of a tanning booth bursting out of her bikini, a statuesque blonde delivered her standup eyeball to eyeball into the camera's lens with all the authority and presence a producer could demand. Karen Carns' presence and personality won her the job even though she was neither a journalist nor a strong news reader.

I have two fond memories of Carns. The morning she was due to report for work I found her sitting on top of her desk looking like something the cat dragged in. She was sick and on her way to the hospital emergency room. When I asked why she didn't just call, she replied, "I just wanted you to see that I was really sick." More often than not Carns wore low-cut blouses that created a major problem for the audio man. There was no convenient fabric upon which to clip a mike. When that happened we gave her a roll of duct tape and told her to stick the mike to her bare chest. Whatever it takes!

Our viewers were genuinely attracted to Carns, who made friends easily and actually baby-sat for some of her fans. She met her future husband in Greensboro before she was recruited away to Minneapolis. Karen later anchored in Salt Lake City and Phoenix.

Vicki Babu: 1982-84

Vicki Babu brought a spritely energy to the "Good Morning Show" plus the anchor credibility we wanted on the news desk. In that era the women co-hosts produced our four newscasts by themselves. It took exceptional management ability to organize the news and look pretty presenting it, but Babu handled the challenge. She was planning her wedding when she arrived for work on the show and our viewers loved to hear us banter about her preparations. The wedding video proved to be a big hit. When an anchor job opened on the 11 p.m. news, Babu decided to go for it. I didn't want her to leave, but she did and the assignment was disastrous. Vicki and David Niswonger and their two children live in St. Louis where she's a news anchor. Kim Skeen, who replaced Vicki, had some nice words for her predecessor:

"It wasn't until Vicki Babu joined the "Good Morning Show" as the fourth co-host that the role of woman began to evolve. Vicki had more experience in news gathering and production in the field. She was also attractive and personable. She easily filled the 'traditional' expectations for the female anchor, sex appeal and energy, but she also added a journalistic dimension to the job."

Kim Skeen: 1984-89

We recruited this University of Georgia Phi Beta Kappa graduate from an anchor-producer position in Augusta. Skeen's experience was the key to an even stronger news image for the "Good Morning Show." She was professionally focused and determined to succeed regardless of the hurdles she had to leap. She inherited the do-it-yourself news producing-anchoring from Babu with no editorial or technical assistance beyond what our director provided.

Hair in curlers, feet in slippers, Skeen got to the newsroom around 3:30 and worked her way through the usual maze of news stories from various sources, including calls to area law enforcement agencies, or "cop shops."

Her great mornings were the ones when the teletypes were operating and there was enough material to produce a newscast. The bad ones occurred when the news machines were off-line and out of paper and we couldn't find the news tapes from the previous day. More often than not, as Skeen pointed out, the "Good Morning Show's" women anchors had to make a choice between the news and themselves, between cosmetics and journalism:

"I must confess that my own fascination with television news has probably fueled the enlargement of the woman's role on the 'GMS'. I have at times even neglected being pretty and likable at the expense of getting the story. Women no longer adorn the set for decoration. We are pressured more than men to be physically attractive, but we may feel proud that our work is finally gaining the journalistic respect it deserves."

Kim is an award-winning investigative reporter for WJLA in Washington, D.C.

Tracy Wilson: 1991-96

Tracy Wilson joined the "Good

Morning Show" from a reporter-week-end anchor position at WWAY-TV in Wilmington. The world's most motivated woman showed up for her job interview at 4:00 a.m. pleading to write that morning's newscasts. She wasn't content to sit and observe. Wilson turned out to be as focused, tough and relentless as Skeen, but with more confrontational fighting spirit. She was an extremely attractive young woman. One of our guests described her this way: "Tracy Wilson is very pretty, very pleasant and has a marvelous complexion. Talk about peaches and cream!"

Wilson's father is a retired hockey-player coach so she was trained in the trenches to over-achieve. She had an extra-hours work ethic that would kill a team of horses. When she joined the show she kept her mouth shut as long as she could and then she criticized everything we did, but she also fought for the show and she worked for it as if she owned it, so I let her make programming decisions. I trusted her and everything she did was in the show's best interest. I knew she would leave someday, but I didn't want it to be in

my lifetime. It was. She resigned in late 1996 to join the 1999 World Special Olympics as their International Spokesperson.

Staci Elgin: 1996-97

I had total chemistry with Tracy Wilson and zero compatibility with Staci Elgin. After a brief stint at co-hosting, we discovered that Staci's strengths lay in beauty and physical fitness segments as well as live spot news and feature reporting.

Kim Jenkins: 1997

One year I was competing against Kim Jenkins and the next year I was welcoming her as co-host of the "Good Morning Show." We're happy to have her presence on our side of the street. Jenkins is deceptively clever, all that Southern demureness and charm can splinter into unpredictable hilarity in an instant. She is a genuinely nice person and I happily anticipate working with her for many years. Observably Kim is unflappable. I've watched her work her way through some awkward situations and enjoyed her sense of self control. Her strongest point is her unrelenting sense of tormenting humor.

The Guy Side

Before I talk about the male co-hosts let me say a few words about chemistry and concept since I have generally described those cases where the combination didn't work. Chemistry is a synonym for compatibility and trust. First, the co-hosts have to be near the same level of intelligence and interests. Second, they have to trust that neither will diminish the other, and, third, they have to support and strengthen each other. If compatibility occurs the viewers will see it happening and approve. If the chemistry doesn't jell the hosts are miserable, the uncomfortable audience squeezes the clicker and we're history. Successful anchor teams are composed of professional broadcasters who feel comfortable with themselves. The camera does not automatically make any presenter a "star." It takes a deep and abiding understanding of what the "presentation of self" is all about.

The team concept is vitally important to the "Good Morning Show" and that's why self-assured personalities are important to the program's health. No member of the team is a "morning person." We don't lie in bed all night just waiting to jump out of the covers in front of the camera. We're groggy, sometimes slow, headachey, sniffly, stiff and there are many days we need to have a warm and wonderful relationship with our colleagues to survive. Okay, let's dissect the guys and see what makes them tick.

Brad Jones: 1995-

Brad Jones is the ultimate broadcast journalist. Before we worked together, the book on Brad read something like this: witty, bright, hard worker, demands excellence, is always well-prepared, a solid professional. He is exceptionally talented, a funny, funny man who could do stand-up comedy, play the guitar and cater the party. Brad has this wonderful knack for seeing challenges from unique perspectives. He is always in good humor, is genuinely a good man, husband and father, great fun to tease and his ideas contribute immeasurably to the "Good Morning Show."

John Nesbit

John Nesbit: 1981-87

Brad reminds me a lot of John Nesbit, the "Good Morning Show's" first male co-host. John was "home-grown-talent" who learned his trade on the job. Nesbit was a critical listener with Brad's knack for questioning what most people casually accept or take for granted. John and I capitalized on this strength and our differing positions on topics to set up some lively "breakfast table opinion" discussions that drew viewers into the fray.

We often debated intensely but our discussions never reached the personal level. If John crunched my wide-ranging generalizations he heard from my fans. If his supporters felt I was overbearing toward the youngster I heard from them. The years John was on the show were the happiest "Good Morning Show" years of my life. After scuba diving became John's passion he left the show to open a "dive" shop in Greensboro. A few years ago he relocated to California where he is an executive with the Professional Association of Diving Instructors.

Mike Hogewood:1988-89

When he joined the "Good Morning Show" Mike Hogewood was a towering inferno of exploding energy. He understands show business as the cult of the personality. He knows how to seize the moment and turn every spontaneous event into a "bit." Mike can be

Mike Hogewood

Mike's forte is the ascerbic commentary which generally irritates about 50 percent of his audience. The first offhand criticism he passed out on the "Good Morning Show" rang his phone off the hook. Hogewood criticized Michael Jackson before it became the popular thing to do! Mike will tell you that the most important thing he learned on the "Good Morning Show" was "how to listen." He credits that with making him a better interviewer. Hogewood is in the midst of a fantastic sports career that keeps expanding with new opportunities, but his first love is the "Good Morning Show" and I have to keep the door locked to stop him from taking over.

Doug Allred: 1990-95

Ellerbee native Doug Allred joined the "Good Morning Show" as sports anchor in March 1990. Tracy Wilson recommended him as a professional who would fit our needs for a multi-talented swing-man to handle studio and field producing and reporting. As a confirmed news reporter Doug was as stiff as a board until we uncovered his puckish personality and provided him op-

intense, hyper and controversial. He is also a multi-talented song-and-dance man who can easily transform himself into an entertainer. Performers like Hogewood can drive a producer totally insane unless you give them a stage wider than life to play on.

portunities to exploit it. When WFMY-TV premiered "Good Morning Weekend," Doug was selected as lead anchor, but he also spends time producing features for the "Good Morning Show." When it comes to taking advantage of opportunities to exploit a live situation Doug is superb.

Ed Matthews: 1995: Meteorologist

Ed Matthews' assignment as "Good Morning Show" meteorologist marked the end of my weather forecasting tenure. Thank heavens! Matthews' dedication to his job, his knowledge of the weather as a Piedmont native and his intensity have established the "Good Morning Show" weather as second to none in the market. Ed was born and raised in Sanford and graduated from N.C. State. He brings a jolly presence to the show excepting those days when his computer, or some fragment of the myriad technology he operates fails. Then he becomes a bear and we are forced to restore his equilibrium by showering him with tender loving care.

Matthews is so intensely focused he often needs to be reminded to relax. When he gets grumpy we send him home to Sanford for a big bowl of his Mother's collard greens. He worries constantly about our viewers, apologizing for threatening their weekends with showers and counseling them not to change their plans because the weather is going to be lousy. He doesn't have the slightest idea how good he really is and there is no questioning his commitment to his profession.

TV Personalities Have Biological Parents

Viewers may not realize how unremittingly personal professional broadcasting, the presentation of self—indeed the risk of self—is to a self-conscious performer. A great performer is a delicate construct. Hosting with colleagues on TV is comparable to performing in any workplace. If you have the right partner or team you excel. When the chemistry doesn't work show business doesn't happen. When the right decisions about co-hosts have been made before they are assigned to the show, the chemistry has worked and nobody knows that better than the viewer. The successful shows are the ones where viewers feel comfortable with a cast that is easy to watch.

Beyond the art of performing, the "Good Morning Show" co-hosts have been splendid young professionals with fine characters. I have watched them mature on the program and enjoyed, most of the time, their brash, know-it-all, I-am-in-control, I-can-do-anything-you-can-do-better attitudes. I have encouraged them to expand their talents, enlarge their lives, stretch themselves. Most of them can do everything I do better than I do and that's the type of performer I appreciate. I need the people I work with to stretch me to a higher level and think more succinctly and precisely. I have learned from them and I celebrate their accomplishments. There has never been a personal or professional failure among the "Good Morning Show" alumni and I'm proud of them all.

NINE

Community Service

The Kinard family at home in the late '60s. From left to right: Beverly, Valerie, Lee, Lee III, and Anne.

When it comes to service I can not separate my life from the history of the "Good Morning Show." If this turns you off I'm sorry, but the program is as close to a ministry as I can get. I believe that a "good" local television program should serve the community and work with its viewers to enhance the quality of life. Community service was built into the "Good Morning Show's" original format and the time devoted to nurturing public needs expanded with the program's broadcast day. This commitment could not have happened had community service not been an integral part of the foundation of WFMY-TV.

The "Good Morning Show" is a "good" local TV program in that it has fostered an intimate relationship with its viewers. The hosts and production personnel assigned to the show are young women and men who are first citizens of the communities in which they live. They have not been transients living apart from the audience they inform, but residents establishing personal roots and friendships, seeking out churches and volunteer projects. They have been parents sending their children to Piedmont schools, joining soccer leagues and the Girl and Boy Scouts.

The professionals who produce and present the "Good Morning Show" understand they are a part of the news they broadcast, be it good or bad, exciting, sad, or frustrating. The folks who work on the program behind or in front of the cameras can't afford to live in ivory towers. They live down the street, around the corner, or in the same apartment complex as the viewers they serve. Many of them have bought their first homes and welcomed their first babies in the Piedmont. They are accessible in the drug store, the supermarket, the flea market and at the kid's soccer game.

We understand that as local broadcasters it is incumbent upon us to be active, involved citizens. We are a continuing presence in classrooms throughout the area and have spoken at numerous D.A.R.E. graduations. We have Grand Marshalled parades, addressed civic clubs and keynoted hundreds of fund raisers. We have walked, ridden, run and bowled for charity, and have begged for and donated blood.

The "Good Morning Show's" history does not contain a long, prestigious list of national honors, or Emmys because we just haven't entered prominent contests. In many cases it was too much trouble to plod through the paperwork, prepare entries and pay the entrance fees. In most cases there aren't categories for what we have provided through a consistency of service. We have been too preoccupied fulfilling our commitment to the Piedmont. Essentially and practically, the "Good Morning Show" has contributed what broadcast media in the United States of America should provide—solid information, not just a vapid list of numerical tips.

Our moral and ethical icons are trustworthiness, commitment and ser-

vice. We function proactively specializing in solving, assisting, reinforcing, subsidizing, and raising cold hard cash for viable projects. There is no computing how many millions of dollars the "Good Morning Show" has raised for PTAs, churches, colleges and universities, disease foundations and individuals who needed help.

Performing community service at a fever pitch helped the show maintain its ratings—which says as much about the culture and needs of our Piedmont audience as it does about the "Good Morning Show." The community access provided by this program and WFMY-TV has never been surpassed by any so-called access channel. We have helped small groups and large, and none has ever been turned away because of its lack of "clout" or its ethnicity.

There are some major achievements of which we are duly proud. They include the "School Days" segments we began presenting in the early '70s when Greensboro integrated its schools. The series won six School Bell Awards from the North Carolina Association of Educators for conveying the message that African-American and white children could learn in harmony.

The "Good Morning Show" has boosted countless literacy programs, but our most successful partnership is with Reading Connections, Inc. This non-profit organization matches students with tutors and creates successes that will make you cry with joy. Jennie Pinnix, an African-American grandmother, is a beautiful example of how learning to read dramatically enriches the lives of sensitive, loving people.

"Now, Lee," Jennie began, "because you told me on TV that Reading Connections would help me learn to read I can now read my Bible. I can read a story to my grandchild while she sits on my lap. It is the most wonderful feeling in the world."

That is what TV should do—change and enhance lives in a positive fashion. It is a source of pride that the "Good Morning Show" was performing educational and community service while Marshall McLuhan was theorizing about a similar mission for TV. On those occasions when the station was sold or a new general manager was ap-

pointed I've been asked to justify the amount of community service the program provides, but few could argue with a commitment that saves lives and families. Thus far none has.

One morning, as she tells it, one of my viewers was at wit's end; her family's desperate need for suitable housing had driven her to the brink of suicide. She decided to kill herself. The act was imminent. Before that final moment she went to tell her family goodbye. My voice on the TV stopped her. I was giving a telephone number distressed families could call for housing assistance. Instead of committing suicide she called the number on her TV screen. Sometime later during a live interview on the "Good Morning Show" she looked me in the face and said, "Lee Kinard, you saved my life!"

Do you understand how fulfilling it is to produce a program that changes people's lives by showing them new possibilities and new directions? Consider the threads that are returned to the fabric of our splintered communities. The "Good Morning Show" puts people in touch with people. We are the support group for viewers who need nourishment, assistance and ideas to make them think about changing their lives.

Most of my viewers are aware that I went back to college as an adult and that I promote the benefits of GEDs and higher education. I am thrilled in Lexington, Reidsville, or Asheboro, when viewers walk up and tell me they decided to complete their education and pursue new opportunities. Their rally cry seems to be "if Lee Kinard can do it, I can do it." Working on the "Good Morning Show" changed my life to a degree that I would never have considered possible.

In the Monday, May 16, 1988, edition of *The Greensboro News and Record* reporter Jim Schlosser reported that "(Lee) Kinard entered the world of lofty learners Sunday (May 15, 1988) when he received a doctor of education degree during commencement at the University of North Carolina at Greensboro....

"Make no mistake. His is not one of those honorary degrees that colleges often use to flatter politicians and celebrities. Kinard got his doctorate the old-fashioned way. He earned it dur-

ing four years of squeezed-in study while serving as host of Channel 2's 'Good Morning Show' and co-anchoring the evening news."

There is a larger story there than should be told here, but in the wash of emotion that followed graduation I decided to go public with my educational background. I thought perhaps my experience as a high school dropout might motivate similarly-distracted students to continue their studies. WFMY-TV cooperated wholeheartedly. It was a project I could promote on the "Good Morning Show" and across the station's broadcast schedule. This is the message I videotaped:

"When I was growing up I had a lot of problems in school. I really didn't understand what education was all about and the difference knowledge could make in your life. I consecutively failed the seventh, eighth and ninth grades, but then some teachers came to my rescue. They saved my life. If you are having problems in school talk to a teacher, or call me."

I was overwhelmed by the response from anguished relatives and friends pleading for help to stem the tide of this cultural malaise. I was quickly on the road promoting the value of education in schools all across the Piedmont. What I found stunned me. For the most part the educational system seemed to be working, but the family was shattered. In some schools the single-parent ratio was 60 percent, with homes split by drugs, alcohol and divorce. In single-parent working homes and blended-family homes multiple problems prevailed.

I brought this information back to the "Good Morning Show" and as a team we began to attack the problem. We escalated our promotion of drug education; we talked with psychologists and counselors about solutions, and we continued to drive home education as the key, not to success as much as to sheer survival. We publicized programs for the learning and behaviorally disabled as we struggled to put the distressed in touch with aid. I got so wrapped up in the cases I discovered that I completely lost my objectivity.

As one teacher observed, I promoted education by "baring my soul," recalling the harsh realities of growing up with an alcoholic father in an abusive home. This "baring of the soul" business got pretty heavy at times. Some days after I drove away from a school I stopped by the side of the road and cried. Time and again I promised myself that I needed to stop reliving my adolescent terrors, but everywhere I went I was catapulted back in time by kids who were going through the same trials I experienced. I want you to know that being with thousands of kids on a day-to-day basis was a phenomenal experience.

There were a lot of students who turned their lives around. One was Michelle Hazard, a West Davidson senior, who dropped out of school, but decided to return and share her experiences with her peers. "I tell them it's not easy, it's too hard," she said. "I liked Mr. Kinard's talk. I think he made everybody think. His openness and freedom in talking to you was good."

Adam Rickard, a freshman at West Davidson who has briefly dropped out twice, said my talk made him realize someone else had gone through the same problem.

"He knows how it is, he's been

there," he said. "I think I am going to try to finish out school."

"This assembly really helped me," said Lee Kennedy, an East Davidson freshman. "When you have problems you need to take charge and change them."

I wasn't the only "Good Morning Show" person working to prevent dropouts. The rest of the co-hosts were in the battle and the crew was involved as well. These experiences in Piedmont schoolrooms inspired a series of educational commentaries titled Dr. K's Klass. These 90-second talks promote the wonder of knowledge and the process of discovering life.

In 1989 I received the Brotherhood Citation Award from the National Conference of Christians and Jews, a major commendation I share with my "Good Morning Show" colleagues. I was particularly proud to have the award presented by Associate Justice Henry E. Frye of the North Carolina Supreme Court. In 1968 Justice Frye became the first African-American elected to the N.C. General Assembly in this century. In response to my remarks at the awards ceremony The *Greensboro News and Record* presented this editorial:

Words of Warning

In receiving the 1989 Brotherhood Citation Award from the Greensboro chapter of the National Conference of Christians and Jews this week, veteran WFMY-TV anchorman Lee Kinard offered sage advice to his audience. He said that Greensboro and this nation have a long way to go in salvaging our young people and improving race relations.

Kinard should know. A high school dropout who eventually earned a doctoral degree, he devotes much of his free time to talking to students and urging them to stay in school and off drugs.

But there was a high note of frustration in Kinard's usually low-key delivery Monday night. What is it about our society, he asked, that makes troubled young people seek an escape from reality in drugs? Why are so many of our children getting lost in the shuffle and winding up on the losing end of life? If we do not reach out and salvage this generation of children, he warned, the battle will be lost.

On race relations, Kinard said that while our community talks about harmony, there are still fundamental problems. Talk is not often transformed into action that genuinely brings different races of people together. Once again, he's right. For all its proud civil rights history, Greensboro still remains a racially-divided town.

Thanks for the candid remarks, Lee. We needed to hear them. Now we need to do something about them.

Human relations and education were two themes the "Good Morning Show" continued to promote into the 1990s. The designation of Martin Luther King Day as a holiday was accepted with mixed emotions in the Piedmont as the *Greensboro News and Record* indicated in its 1990 King holiday edition, but the "Good Morning Show" planned to broadcast the Dr. Martin Luther King, Jr. Prayer Breakfast live.

"WFMY news anchor and 'Good Morning Show' host Lee Kinard says today's Martin Luther King, Jr. holiday underscores principles that are universal.

"'It's an opportunity for all Americans to consider the value of their civil rights,' Kinard says. 'Dr. King wanted to forge a new way for his own people, but that's a feeling that everybody can relate to and share in.

"'It disappoints me that more of our leaders haven't gotten out there and supported this as a day when we can all examine our personal commitment to civil rights.'"

Human relations have been the prime focus of the "Good Morning Show" for many decades, but there are many other worthy projects we have shared with our various communities.

The Pet of the Week is enormously popular. Every Thursday the "Good Morning Show" offers a dog for adoption from the Guilford County Animal Shelter. The response is so overwhelming that adopters often have to draw for the pet, but that's terrific because these kind folks often go home with other animals. The show heartily supports fund raising activities sponsored by the Guilford County Humane Society and promotes spaying and neutering.

The most thrilling community service event the "Good Morning Show" sponsored in its first 40 years was an emergency blood drive in the summer of 1982. Co-host John Nesbit suggested staging the event to cope with a serious blood emergency in the Piedmont. Traditionally, WFMY-TV sponsors the largest bloodmobile collection drive in North Carolina during the Christmas season, but in August 1982 it became apparent that we needed to respond to an unexpected challenge.

With Jo Ann Frazier, the Greensboro Red Cross Blood Program director, the "Good Morning Show" launched a week-long promotion for a special donor collection set for Friday, August 3, 1982. We had a whopping turnout. More than 2,000 people lined up from 10 in the morning until 9 at night. But there was a major glitch; the Red Cross had not planned for the onslaught and early on it became evident that our donor turn-out was surpassing the capacity to collect.

Charles M. Hassell, M.D., director of laboratories at the Moses H. Cone Memorial Hospital in Greensboro, demanded emergency assistance from Red Cross authorities in Charlotte. Hassell organized an emergency staff of medical technologists from the hospital and his private lab. The donor scene was chaotic. Raising hell with me and Nesbit, people stood in line for hours. Many went without lunch and I didn't have sense enough to call up the station and get somebody to make a deal with one of the burger giants to feed the crowd. We could have collected nearly 2,000 units but we ended the day with 1,062. Hassell's "thank you" note to the people of the Piedmont appeared in the *Greensboro Daily News*:

"Over 2,000 volunteers registered to donate blood. They are due a special thanks and many of them are due an apology. They waited from two to four and one half hours in order to donate their blood. Reason? The bloodmobile was understaffed. Quite frankly, the Regional Center in Charlotte underestimated what Greensboro would do. It was a Friday night, summertime, an unscheduled visit, etc. They simply did not recognize the generosity of the media and the responsiveness of the Greensboro people."

• • •

The "Good Morning Show" has been promoting the North Carolina State Zoo since its inception more than 30 years ago. We regularly televise features from the zoo presented by Public Relations Manager Rod Hackney and recorded by videographer George Vaughn. In 1982 WFMY-TV contributed proceeds from the sale of the "Good Morning Show's" 25th Anniversary Commemorative Mug to the zoo.

The "Good Morning Show" has anchored WFMY-TV's exemplary community affairs program managed by Shirley Frye and assisted by Dona Pickett. We have supported the replenishment of our Piedmont Food Banks, the Greensboro Urban Ministry and the Northwest Food Bank of N.C. through WFMY-TV's "Food to Families" promotion. Traditionally we broadcast live from the Greensboro Urban Ministry every Thanksgiving morning as hundreds of restaurant volunteers prepare Thanksgiving dinner for the hungry and homeless. That show also introduces the Annual Greensboro Urban Ministry Honor Card painted by William Mangum.

"The Good Morning Show" is a major supporter of "Tools for Schools," WFMY-TV's pre-school drive for school supplies which helped over 20,000 students in 1996. And of course there is the United Way. Long a champion of the United Way of Greater Greensboro, Inc., the program has supported United Way drives throughout the Piedmont. When the United Way suffered problems with its national image in the '90s "The Good Morning Show" didn't back off. We knew that our local agencies were driven by top quality community volunteers and we stuck with them.

In television you can win or lose in the ratings, but you can never lose if you respect your viewers and contribute information and assistance to their nourishment and well being. Serving your fellow woman and man is still the way to go in this world and commercial TV stations must honor their public obligation by leading and committing.

The "Good Morning Show" is many things to many people. It is a time line, a compendium, a calendar, a schedule, a forecast, a consistent carousel of information, ideas and opinions. It appeals to the distracted and the distressed; to those who need friends and family; it is a warm communal hearth, an umbrella, a canopy. When all is said and done and my "Good Morning Show" days are packed away forever I will foremost remember and revere our community service projects. They are the good we have done and they stand alone as representative of the character of WFMY-TV and the "Good Morning Show."

TEN

Moments of Crisis

Lee at the sight of Pickett's Charge at Seminary Ridge near Gettysburg in 1963.

Since December 16, 1957, the "Good Morning Show" has been a mirror and a lamp for early morning viewers in the Piedmont of North Carolina and Virginia. A mirror because the events of more than four decades have been the top stories locally, nationally and internationally. They include the demonstrations of the civil rights era and the Vietnam War, The Nazi-Klan/Communist Workers shootout and trial, Hurricane Hugo and countless other stories that affected our daily lives.

The "Good Morning Show" is a lamp because the program's mission has always been to inform and suggest options for enhancing life and surviving tragedy, for aiding our viewers, seeing to their safety and comfort. The record of service speaks for itself; on many occasions the "Good Morning Show" led the way and headlined the dawn in crisis situations. Morning after morning since the late '50s the program has been consistently present in the Piedmont.

Sometimes hard news dominates the "Good Morning Show." We're positive journalists, but when tragedy strikes it's our job to report the trauma precisely and objectively and to reassure our viewers as they struggle through pain and anxiety. There are some mornings when hard news is good news, such as the release of our Vietnam POW's from the "Hanoi Hilton," including my childhood pal Quincy Collins. But hard news is often bad news, as on the morning I, unaware at the moment, reported my brother-in-law's death in Vietnam.

The "Good Morning Show" began with the American Space Age and the countdown to the launch of the first Atlas ICBM at Cape Canaveral.

Our first major local top story documented the Woolworth sit-ins on February 1, 1960, a courageous demonstration marking the beginning of a series of memorable civic moments.

The sit-in was the first time my personal life intersected with my professional life. My father grew up in the 5 & 10 chain and managed Woolworth stores in Concord and Beckley, West Virginia. I knew many of the company's executives and wondered how they would react to this landmark protest.

As a journalist I reported daily accounts of the demonstrations on the "Good Morning Show" newscasts. As a citizen and parent I was concerned for the safety of my family. I was aware of bristling African-American dissatisfaction with the humiliation of segregation, but having been raised on stories of Ku Klux Klan atrocities, I was concerned that the sit-ins might precipitate a race war.

The civil rights struggle dominated the local news throughout the '60s, but there were certain hot-spots that boiled to a fever pitch. Between May 11 and June 7, 1963, 18 marches rumbled across downtown Greensboro. Some nights as many as 2,000 demonstrators shouted their way through the central business district. When nearly 1,500 college students and teenagers were jailed, Greensboro's adult African-American population rallied to their support and the protest escalated. Student leaders selected a young football player to spearhead the marches and Jesse Jackson became a prominent newsmaker.

In April, 1968, the assassination of Dr. Martin Luther King, Jr. revived the nightmares of racial violence. Angry demonstrations in downtown Greensboro forced Mayor Carson Bain to call National Guard troops and implement a city-wide curfew. The morning after Dr. King's assassination News 2 reporter Ted Harrison appeared live on the "Good Morning Show" to narrate his dramatic film report on the damage wrought by demonstrators. WFMY-TV did not have live remote broadcast equipment so a reporter on the set marked a first in news coverage.

While Harrison updated the local situation I read wire copy and narrated video of demonstrations occurring across America. To the extreme displeasure of some members of my audience I evidently referred to the slain leader by his last name only; for example, "King said this," or "King did that." During a break in our coverage I learned that more than a dozen callers had threatened to kill me if I didn't identify the slain civil rights leader by his full name and title, Dr. Martin Luther King, Jr.

Spring 1969 saw a new wave of civil violence triggered by an administrative decision at Greensboro's Dudley High School. A joint faculty-student committee denied a civil rights activist's candidacy for student council president. When this controversy spread to the N.C. A & T State University campus National Guard troops arrived in Greensboro again. Early on the morning of May 22, 1969, A & T student Willie Grimes was shot in the head and killed by an unidentified assailant. A few hours later as troops swept through the predominantly black campus, I was reacting to news from another war zone.

"(SAIGON) THREE AMERICAN PLANES HAVE BEEN INVOLVED IN AN AIR COLLISION DURING A REFUELING OPERATION 400 MILES NORTH OF SAIGON. A MARINE JET FIGHTER-BOMBER COLLIDED WITH AN AERIAL TANKER AND A SECOND FIGHTER-BOMBER WAS HIT BY FRAGMENTS FROM THE COLLISION. ALL THREE PLANES FELL INTO THE SOUTH CHINA SEA. TWO CREWMEN WERE RESCUED AND A SEARCH IS UNDERWAY FOR EIGHT OTHERS BELIEVED ABOARD THE PLANES WHICH COLLIDED.

"AN AMERICAN SPOKESMAN SAYS THE CAUSE OF THE COLLISION HAS NOT BEEN DETERMINED."

When I read this story on a "Good Morning Show" newscast I was unaware that my brother-in-law, Major Jimmy D. Sells of Richfield, was piloting the doomed aerial tanker. I loved my brother-in-law. This was a devastating personal tragedy for our family and doubly distressing to drive out of the city to Jim's memorial service in Norfolk through a cordon of National Guardsmen protecting Greensboro's citizens from each other.

The '60s and '70s were the incessantly plodding years for the "Good Morning Show." I'd present the weather, news and sports every half hour and then interview the day's guests. I was sandwiched between civil rights demonstrations on the homefront and the Vietnam War's casualty lists. My best childhood friend, Air Force flyer Quincy Collins, was imprisoned in the notorious POW camp called "Hanoi Hilton." Jimmy Sell's violent accidental death and the pervasive pain and anguish over the war in America that nobody seemed capable of solving or mediating just made me sick, but still I had to read the dreary news and read it and read it.

The next crisis emerged following the Nazi-Klan/Communist Workers shootout when a whole new technological era was driving TV news coverage. In November, 1979, electronic newsgathering made it more convenient than ever to exploit news events like the Morningside Homes bloodbath. Because videographers were present, the tragedy's 88 terrifying seconds are thoroughly documented. The best published account of the story that turned the "Good Morning Show" toward a new community service mission is Elizabeth Wheaton's *Codename Greenkil: The 1979 Greensboro Killings* (1987).

On November 3, 1979, members of the Communist Workers Party staged a "Death to the Klan" rally in Morningside Homes, a predominantly African-American housing development in Greensboro. When members of the Ku Klux Klan invaded the demonstration a gun battle erupted. When the firing ended after 88 hair-raising seconds, five demonstrators were dead or dying and nine were wounded.

This incident and the African-American community's reaction to it posed tremendous implications for Greensboro's leaders and its citizens. Confronting city officials was a monstrous human relations problem that threatened further conflict. The fact that the killings had taken place in a predominantly black community was the major issue. I must emphasize that while this shooting involved a host of people from outside Greensboro the very fact that it happened where it did, and how it did, in Greensboro impacted mightily on white and African-American human relations.

I wanted the "Good Morning Show" to play a major role in reinforcing racial harmony in the city. In addition to producing the "Good Morning Show" I was also deeply involved in supervising the station's community affairs section. Melding these roles I searched for strategies and TV content to restore mutual respect and trust. The milestone I decided to capitalize on as a celebratory community moment was the forthcoming 20th Anniversary of the Woolworth sit-ins slated for February 1, 1980.

My prime contact for approving and arranging live coverage of this memorial was Shirley Frye, wife of North Carolina Supreme Court Justice Henry Frye, and a member of the February One Committee. Mrs. Frye's committee was promoting the 20th observance of the lunch counter sit-ins at the original site. On February 1, 1980, Greensboro's downtown Woolworth was jammed with national and local press, but the "Good Morning Show" was the only program televising the commemoration live.

After the four original sit-in participants sat down on their historical stools I interviewed Ezell Blair, Jr., Joseph McNeil, David Richmond and Franklin McCain. While we reminisced about youthful daring and courageous decision-making, members of the 1960 Woolworth wait staff graciously passed out coffee and donuts. Blair, McNeil, Richmond and McCain reviewed their experiences simply and sometimes humorously. They remembered themselves as four nervous young students, men of the moment, committed to changing the way they were treated in the United States of America. They were youngsters beginning a non-violent protest that radically altered American society.

However positive my intentions were in televising the 20th Anniversary commemoration of the sit-in the project fell on deaf ears in at least one Greensboro home. A viewer responded:

"When are you TV people ever going to stop talking about that mess at Woolworth? Haven't they got all the publicity they want out of that mess. Since they can eat anywhere they want why don't they just shut up about it all. Me and all the white people I know are sick of hearing about it."

The Sit-In Anniversary keynoted the "Good Morning Show's" coverage of Black History Month. With the trial of those who had perpetrated the Nazi-

Klan/Communist Workers Shootout still months away, the prevailing tension was an imperative for strengthening cultural understanding. This difficult period equaled the tensions surrounding the assassination of Dr. Martin Luther King, Jr. African-American and white alliances that had been strongly forged in a decade of dialogue were once again suspect. They needed strengthening as the date of the Nazi-Klan trial approached.

The "Good Morning Show" commemoration of Black History Month began with a series on the African Heritage Cultural Museum at N.C. A & T State University. Since the "Nazi-Klan/Communist Shootout" had raised questions about operations within the Greensboro Police Department, we scheduled a weekly series to discuss the department's organization and mission and Greensboro psychologist John Edwards presented a series on the psychological aspects of racial prejudice in Greensboro.

Our guest-list included a number of prominent African-American leaders including Andrew Young, a former Congressman and U.S. Ambassador to the U.N. Young was preparing the Atlanta mayoral campaign he won in 1981. I interviewed the Rev. Leon White of the N.C. Commission on Racial Justice and Ben Chavis of the "Wilmington Ten." N.C. A & T State University students promoted a thematic interracial play and we showcased the University Choir. In a campaign to raise representative awareness the "Good Morning Show" heavily publicized the NAACP's voter registration drive.

The Nazi-Klan trial began August 11, 1988. Instinctively, many Greensboro citizens were apprehensive about its outcome, fearing violence should an all-white jury find the defendants innocent. This concern was shared by many in the local media. A meeting was convened by TV and Radio broadcasters to reach a consensus on coverage following a verdict in this trial. On two occasions in the autumn of 1980 while the trial was underway we met quietly at the Greensboro City Club.

At the second meeting invited city officials revealed their contingency plans should demonstrations flare following an innocent verdict. We agreed to a simple but objective reportorial process. After verification the verdict would be presented calmly and factually without editorial comment. If confrontations or demonstrations did occur, they would be thoroughly verified and reported objectively and unemotionally.

Predictably the three-month trial ended with a verdict of innocent. The decision reached the media at 5:30 p.m. on the evening of November 17, 1980, in a cold, blinding rainstorm. As the deluge droned its wet, weary way into history no major incidents were reported. Perhaps the tension had been diluted by the storm. Perhaps Greensboro's African-Americans had given up on justice. Perhaps the feverish leadership of the '60s had disappeared. Perhaps a modicum of economic and social mobility had distanced socially-mobile African-American leaders from their folk in Morningside Homes. Perhaps civic responsibility succeeded in defusing what many imagined as disastrous.

For all of these hypotheses, or none of them, Greensboro was not plunged into chaos. Former Greensboro Mayor Jim Melvin recalled the part the "Good Morning Show" played in the aftermath of the Shootout and the "Nazi-Klan" trial:

"I strongly feel that the communication obtained by appearing on your show was one of the strongest, positive things we did while I was mayor. Through the opportunity to be on the 'GMS' and have some extended period of time to discuss important issues, the citizens of our area were much better informed concerning the things that were happening in our community. It also gave us an opportunity to address some of the problems, and I specifically mean the situation during the Nazi/Klan/Communist Workers Party incident.

"The year of high tension in our community that was experienced after the incident was helped a great deal by the fact that we were able to appear on your show from time to time to discuss the critical points involved with that issue.

"In my opinion the 'Good Morning Show' is truly one of the great communication vehicles in modern communications today. I don't know of any other community that has had the opportunity to have a show whose sole premise is to communicate the many happenings in the region to its viewing audience which, I am convinced, is why your ratings stay so high. People realize that by watching your show they will have a good feel for many of the things going on in their community."

In 1979 social activists and violent strangers picked Greensboro to settle their hatred savaging a decade of intense human relations negotiations. African-Americans were deeply incensed that such a tragedy could have occurred in one of their neighborhoods. It gave them reasons to believe that the human relations gap in Greensboro had not been bridged. Whites, on the other hand, couldn't understand the blacks' anger over violence that appeared to have nothing to do with the city. For whites the "Death To The Klan Rally" was an outside-promoted event that backfired.

As Historian William Chafe pointed out in *Civilities and Civil Rights* (1981):

"The demonstration represented an effort to provide dramatic focus to an ongoing attempt to build a bi-racial, class-based struggle against the textile magnates and bankers whom CWP [Communist Workers Party] members saw as the primary enemies of social and economic justice. Frustrated by their failure to make rapid strides in mobilizing workers, CWP members hoped that a highly-publicized march against the Klan might provide a vehicle to attract new recruits. Consequently, they challenged Klan leaders to appear at the rally and 'answer the people's' judgment. Arriving with a virtual arsenal of weapons, KKK and Nazi party members, after a brief scuffle, opened fire on CWP followers. Eighty-eight seconds later five CWP demonstrators lay dead."

The Nazi-Klan/Communist Workers Shootout and trial were pervasive ongoing stories permeating the "Good Morning Show" day-in, day-out with routine, incessant follow-ups. Viewers who object to repetition have the luxury of tuning out, but we don't. We have to stay with the story as depressing as it may be. In this case WFMY-TV utilized the "Good Morning Show" to promote racial harmony and I am proud to have been a part of that mission. However, there have been times when I have allowed my objectivity to be blown away.

On January 28, 1985, the Space Shuttle Challenger exploded immediately after an 11:38 a.m. lift-off from Cape Kennedy. It killed seven astronauts, including school teacher Christa McAuliffe, the first private citizen picked for a space flight. When this tragic accident occurred I was in bed battling a severe case of the flu. I was stricken, not only by McAuliffe's death, but by that of Astronaut Major Ronald McNair.

Dr. McNair was a graduate of N.C. A & T State University. Not many months before his death I had hosted and produced a live program from downtown Greensboro when the city and his alma mater saluted his achievements with a special ceremony. McNair's prestige positively boosted his university, Greensboro, North Carolina and the nation. I was as distraught over McNair's death as I was McAuliffe's and I attached this misery to a local topic that was really getting on my nerves.

The Greensboro-Guilford County school merger issue was simmering and my involvement with the public schools clouded my journalistic judgment. On Friday, January 30, I struggled back to the show from the flu before I should have; frustrated by the Challenger tragedy and what I personally considered to be both bureaucratic and racist views on the local school merger question, I proceeded to ad-lib a tirade that mushroomed into a minor controversy. You can detect my mental struggle within the context of the transcription from the videotape of that show:

"Something has been bugging me ever since this space shuttle blew up and I need to say something about it this morning, 'cause this thing about the teacher on board—Christa McAuliffe, you know—and all of a sudden over all these years in the U.S. we've had this big debate about schools and about teachers, and we have an educational system in this country that was built by the early philosophers to reinforce the democratic ideals that this country was built on—but in the process of everything all kinds of politics have gotten mixed up in the situation, so that somehow through the years the focus of the fact that we take little babies who are four to five years old and try to in some way educate them. An awful lot of people out there have an awful lot of ideas and some of these ideas are very good and some are very selfish and one would hope now that this teacher going on the mission into space has died that somehow or other in somebody's eyes or mind or heart, that might cause some kind of rededication to take place so that we won't be selfish anymore.

"Look at North Carolina. We've got too many school systems and too many people are selfish about maintaining those school systems when some school systems really ought to merge and we've got other people who are saying well maybe we ought to let people play ball or sing in choruses when they don't make the kind of grades they need to make to pass to reach that point of achievement. So, when out there, when do you start to stop a kid from sliding? How long do you let him slide before you say, you can't slide anymore, now you've got to get your act together? And what about you kids out there who act ugly in your classroom and you don't pay attention

to your teacher and you don't get your lessons done?

"Now this is the time to rededicate yourself. And what about you school systems who've got so many political problems that you can't even hire a superintendent? Don't you think it's about time you got to work and did something about that? You sit here day in and day out for 35 years, you read the news and you get sick and tired of seeing some of the things that happen out there in the public.

"Now this lady is dead. Now the best we can do for her is send condolences to the family and make some kind of a dedicatory effort on our part to see that we got respect for what we are studying and we got respect for our teachers.

"And you teachers out there, the burden is on you too. I think teachers ought to make 35 thousand dollars a year if they are worth it. I don't care if you make 100 thousand dollars a year if you are worth it. I think the state government ought to see that the schools and our children are taken care of to the very "nth" of their ability, to the very best of their ability, and I think it ought to be a number-one priority. And I hope this poor lady's death is going to make somebody think.

"It's all over for her. It happened in a split second. Whether you believe in God or not this lady is all right and she's being taken care of in some other place, but there are an awful lot of kids here who need to be taken care of.

"And what about those of you this morning who walk into the classroom and dedicate yourself, not to just getting out of high school, but going on to get a doctorate and being somebody, and I don't want to ever hear anybody referring to someone whose got a Ph.d. or an Ed.D. as some kind of an egghead because these people have committed to some kind of important inquiry in life like Dr. Ron McNair from A & T State University."

When I screwed up my courage to look at the videotape I saw a sick, angry man staring into the lens and an obviously embarrassed John Nesbit and Kim Skeen who were on the set with me when I launched this resentful, convoluted outburst. After I concluded I apologized like a nice little boy who had just talked out of turn, who

lost his temper and was sorry if he had hurt anybody's feelings.

The first 60 or so phone calls were solidly positive. I assume they came from my teacher friends, or at least from people who saw the commentary. Then as the morning progressed and what I said, or supposedly said, was traded from conversation to conversation, the negative calls began to come in from people who had only heard about the diatribe. The chairman of the Guilford County Board of Education, who had not seen the commentary, asked for equal time to reply to my merger and superintendent-hiring comments. The merger issue would drift controversially into the 1990s as Greensboro-Guilford County anguished over educational identity and governance.

Months later, a minister remarked in a private conversation, "Lee, about that merger speech you made on the 'Good Morning Show,' I want you to know that you were right. At the core the issue against merger was racism." Fearing that merger would force their children to go to school with African-Americans people in at least one section of Guilford County were particularly vitriolic about the issue. Within a few years merger was effected and a new Guilford County Schools superintendent was hired.

ELEVEN

Letters, We Get Letters

WFMY has staged contests and debates to encourage viewer feedback.

A performer with a thin skin is an endangered species. A viewer's evaluation can be brutally dehumanizing and devastating, but positive cards, letters and calls can make your day. When my colleagues get really distressed I suggest they go to the mall, where it's possible to reinforce your ego based on how many shoppers ID you.

On the downside, unsigned letters and anonymous phone calls are frustrating until you condition yourself to manage them objectively. Frankly, in many cases positive criticism has changed our attitudes and approaches, and convinced us to alter our behavior and reconsider our statements.

If a missive is particularly vitriolic we often phone our critic and confront the issue. Unsigned letters are cheap shots from outright cowards, especially when they are sent to the general manager. For many years I read the unsigned letters and attempted to placate anonymous phone calls, but I don't do that anymore. If you haven't got the guts to tell me your name and number I won't talk with you. I look for a signature on your letter first and an address and if there is neither you've wasted your time.

It is good to know when you have offended people because then you can apologize, but 90 percent of the angry calls we get are from people who didn't "hear" what we were saying, or got their information second hand and just want to start a fight. If viewers are reasonable we can have a dialogue. The unreasonable should pick on somebody their own size.

The letters I've selected encompass a wide range of topics from praise to criticism, from the petty to the pathetic, from cosmetics to politics, from prose to poetry, from disgust to adoration. They are representative and I think you'll find them humorous, spiritual, bewildering and bedeviling. First, a few shaggy dog stories:

Linwood, N.C., Jan. 27, 1981:

My family have been faithful viewers of your "Good Morning Show" for years and years. My older dog always used to howl softly along with your old theme song and do a pretty good job of keeping time with the music. Then when we added two of his pups to the household, they joined in with more gusto, and for the past several years your appearance on television at six o'clock in the morning was a guaranteed howling success in at least one house in the viewing area. That old theme song of yours is the only music that has ever turned them on; your present theme meets only silent indifference. Most folks would probably be relieved, but for us it was a cute trick, and I miss it. I wonder if you could possibly get me a cassette tape recording of your past theme song, so that I could wake them up once in a while.

Graham, July 27, 1977:

A couple of months ago my niece was at the dog pound and found a cat about to be eaten alive by the dogs.

She took the cat home with her and by the "hand me down process" and my soft-hearted husband's weakness for cute, lonely animals this cat made his way into my home. We had a time trying to find a name for the cat, but finally decided on Sam because we had a dog named Sheila.

Sam didn't even answer to his name and we were in search of another name for him when we discovered an unusual hobby of his. He loves your show. Wouldn't miss it for the world. He especially likes the TV 2 color radar. One of these days he's going to catch it, we just know he will, either he'll catch it or we'll be out a TV set. I just wanted you to know that while your radar keeps going round, my cat keeps chasing it and he now has a new name, "Radar," and he answers to this name!

A Cumberland County viewer tuned in from well beyond our viewing area and forwarded a precise critique.

Fayetteville, N.C., May 21, 1975:

I enjoy your 6 a.m. show and have some suggestions.

1. The satellite photo tells more than

lines and letters on a map.

2. Weather news is stretched out too long.

3. Sports news is too little.

eg. This is the way you announce ballgames:

San Francisco 6, Pittsburgh 4,

Los Angeles 3, Chicago 2, etc...too fast.

eg: nothing this morning about NBA playoff last night.

eg: nothing about the Indy 500.

4. Your guests are most disinteresting sometimes, and not at all interesting around the state.

5. Suggestions: More feature film clips, events around the state (not just yours).

Thanks for your program, its the best 6 a.m. program.

Across 40 years the "Good Morning Show" has touched at least three generations and many viewers have adopted us as surrogate family members. In this case I was the man around the house for a lonely service wife and mother:

Mebane, N.C. March 4, 1965:

I first saw your show in 1960 when I returned to N.C. from Las Vegas, Nevada. I was a faithful viewer for the four months I was here until I joined my husband on Okinawa. It was sure nice to hear a man's voice in the house other than Popeye, Huckleberry Hound and Yogi Bear.

Now that I'm back home again waiting to join my husband in the Philippines it was just nice to see your familiar, friendly face on TV again. I wonder if you always feel as good as you look and manage to be in such a good mood so early in the morning. It just makes my day when you break into that smile of yours. And that's my TV for the day. After you I'm too busy for any more and with 4 boys now that look at "Combat," "Rawhide," and "Voyage to the Bottom of the Sea" in the evening, I think I'm entitled to my "GOOD MORNING SHOW" don't you?

Just one more thing and I'll let you get back to work. I really liked the gray jacket you wore this morning. It's really refreshing to see a TV reporter dressed as though he's going somewhere besides a funeral. Thanks for lending your ear to a temporary widow.

• • •

Once upon a time in TV land there existed a decorum born of conservative Southern "raisin'." There were certain words and topics that were not discussed before a TV audience or in public. I was personally embarrassed the first time I had to say "whore" on TV and I prayed Mother wasn't watching the morning I committed this sinful act while interviewing a representative from a local theater group. A viewer's letter:

The one program I thought I wouldn't have any trouble with was "The Good Morning Show" and I have been looking at it for years. I truly admire you.

I was very upset with the review or interview of "The Best Little Whorehouse in Texas."

My young daughter does not know what the word "whore" means and I was hoping to wait a little longer before having to explain.

I'm sure there were other movies that could have been talked about. I am very disappointed. I am beginning to think, what next?

Surely, you could have a say in this.

I am still trying to decide if this next viewer wanted me to buy them a new TV after theirs expired!

Coleridge, N.C., Sept. 14, 1976:
We miss seeing your station's programs so much. Our TV went up in smoke and flame when we went to plug it in the wall our second one to burn out, the wiring here where we rent an apt. is very bad defective so we don't want any TV's here again, we miss seeing your wonderful programs.

We get more positive viewer comments on the "Good Morning Show" travel segments than on any other features, but that doesn't imply they are universally accepted. After making her point this viewer was still interested in purchasing one of our 25th anniversary commemorative coffee mugs, so I guess we kept her in the fold.

Sanford, N.C., 1982:
I have been watching the "GOOD MORNING SHOW" for as long as I can remember. I really do enjoy your show.

It is very informing and entertaining. But, Mr. Kinard, I have one complaint, as of lately all you have on there is some thing about Germany. I have seen it so much I feel like I have been there & I am tired of it. So please try to go somewhere else for a change! How could I get one of those "Good Morning Show" mugs?

When John Nesbit co-hosted the "Good Morning Show" in the '80s we haggled over a host of issues and "dug" each other playfully as family members often do. Occasionally the viewers were prone to take sides.

High Point, N.C., February 26, 1982:

Friday morning we finally got John (Nesbit) back to give a decent sports report, and when he got through you griped because it was too long. I just wanted you to know the reason we tune in each morning to hear news, weather and sports. Not your reports of Paris or whatever. To us sports are far more important and interesting, to others they might like the Paris films but I say let's divide it equally. How long did your clip last, as long as the sports?

Again, I say it's good for John to be back and I thought you were very rude to him. Not everybody looks at things like Lee Kinard. Your smart remarks to John, not only cuts him down, but it sure makes you look small and it doesn't make Channel 2 look too good for an older man to put down a young man right there on TV because he gave the only sports report we've had in a long time.

Nesbit is the consummate environmentalist. As the Atlantic Ocean wore away our state's barrier islands we discussed efforts to save the famed Cape Hatteras lighthouse from the encroaching sea.

Bear Creek, N.C. July 30, 1982:

I would like to express my disappointment in yours and John's (Nesbit) attitude about the repair needed to preserve the lighthouse at Cape Hatteras. After seeing the film of your visits to other countries I can't imagine you wanting to see the lighthouse destroyed. What if this attitude was taken about the pyramids of Egypt?

I have been watching Channel 2 for a long time but may switch to 5 if you continue being so muleheaded!

John and I agreed that the Cape Hatteras lighthouse should be left to the mercy of the sea. We were opposed to building barriers to save it, but our Bear Creek friend had her way. The monument is safely barricaded and for the moment will not fall prey to the whip-sawing waves rushing shoreward from the Graveyard of the Atlantic.

A school teacher was trained by our program to observe a more personal priority.

July 30, 1987, Greensboro:
I can honestly say that I grew up with the "Good Morning Show." My mother likes to tell the story of how as a baby, the "Good Morning Show" helped to potty-train me. She would set up the portable training potty in front of the TV with the "Good Morning Show" on and leave me there until my business was finished.

*As I got older the "Good Morning Show" was still there. As a junior and senior in high school I drove an el-*ementary school bus which meant I had to leave the house by 7 a.m. each morning. You were always there to tell me how cold it was and how much frost there was so that I would know how early I needed to go out and start the bus to defrost or warm up. You were also always there to let me know if I didn't need to start the route because of snow or ice that had closed the schools.*

Now as an adult and career woman you are still there helping me by giving me the latest news, weather and any other information that I need to get the day started right. I get up by 6 a.m. so I can see the show. My whole day is ruined if I miss any part of it. I have three TV's in my house and they are usually always on in the morning so whatever room I am in, I can still see/ hear what's happening on the show.

Please never, never stop being the kind of show that you are and please also know that you are very much a part of my family and my life.

Occasionally, we receive sad, un-explainable letters from viewers appar-ently beyond the mainstream, but with a strong sense of conviction like this somber note from a World War I veteran.

Channel 2 WFMY-TV
Greensboro, N.C.
Has a good host for the Good Morning Show, and I like his program, and I believe that he means good, but I do not believe that he gets the correct answer to some of his questions?
At one time my name was: Private (blank)
Company I 30 Division
Serial Number: (blank)
Served with honor in World War I, and wounded in action.
Signed Woodrow Wilson, President of the United States.
It was a great woe for me to walk on the dead, it was a great woe for me to leave my buddies dead on the battlefield, in a dark and dreadful night I heard the firing of a long range gun, and heard the shell coming, and when the shell hit the ground, I heard a soldier scream, and call the Lord and his mother, this was a great woe for me. After an angel from heaven binds Satan the devil for a thousand years, there will be no more soldiers screaming and calling the Lord and their mother. (Until then the kings of the earth will keep lying about peace). I like Greensboro for some of my good friends have lived in Greensboro, and some of my war buddies in World War One were from Greensboro.
My wife tells me that my spelling is bad, and for this time I am saying many thanks for your "Good Morning Show."

That letter included more than a dozen Bible quotations relating to war, peace, and Armageddon. It reached the program in the closing days of the Vietnam War and is indicative of how people of faith in the Bible Belt reacted to our discussions surrounding this conflict in the latter '60s and early '70s.

Children have always been important to the "Good Morning Show." They have been known to control the sets in their homes in the morning, so we cater to them at every opportunity.

Winston Salem, July 31, 1987:
Our oldest son is 27 years old now, but when he was 4 or 5 years old we

watched channel 2 all the time. In fact we watched your channel so much that our son told everyone he lived in Greensboro. He really thought he did cause that's the only city he ever heard mentioned on TV. When he started school, his teacher had a terrible time convincing him that he lived in Winston-Salem.

Blessed are the ties that bind viewers to the "Good Morning Show" especially at an early age.

Winston Salem, July 1, 1964:
I had to write to tell you about our little two-year-old daughter Betsy Anne. She has fallen in love with you. She doesn't want anyone to appear on TV but you. She can't understand why you are not on all the time. We first thought that we were hearing things when she started crying for Lee Kinard. As a rule, she only cares for Casper or Yogi Bear. You probably think this is silly, but we can't get over the effect you have had on her.

School and educational topics provoked a mixed response from our audience. While most weather emergencies we covered dealt with ice and snow storms, the dismissal of students during abnormally hot periods in the late spring or early summer was a steamy topic. However, this viewer was obviously more concerned with her own oppression than that of innocent, sweaty school children.

Asheboro, September 16, 1987:
Dear Lee
I've been a regular fan of the Good Morning Show for a long time but I cannot continue to listen to this program while getting ready for work.
My entire day is ruined everytime school issues are discussed on that program. This morning put the icing on the cake. This is the second time I have heard the suggestion that school houses be air conditioned. This is the biggest farce of all time for wasting taxpayers' money. The mere mention of air conditioning buildings that will stand vacant during most of June, all of July and most of August is downright comical. When one considers how much time these students are off on vacation during the months they are sup-

posed to be in school, it is even more ridiculous.

It seems to me they would spend more time in school during the months that school is supposed to be in operation so they would not have to go during the summer months at all.

It bothers me even more when I am trying to be nice to the public, answer phones, do the secretarial work and all the bookkeeping for two corporations in a metal building with almost no air conditioning, and the temperature hovers around 85 to 90 degrees in the afternoons. As if that isn't enough, I have to go straight to another bookkeeping job when I leave here so I can pay in all those taxes to be so flippantly wasted by schools and other organizations thought up by our government officials.

The bottom line is—if schools are going to be air conditioned at fantastic cost to the tax papers, then students should be in school during the summer months to justify the expense.

We have all been affected by the technological revolution, but I'm still trying to comprehend the severity of the following crisis:

Greensboro, 11/2/81:

Lee, This is an unverified story of how a computer was use (sic) to resolve a human problem.

When misunderstandings resulted whenever the ambassadors from Oman and Saudi Arabia and South Yemen spoke to each other in Mahri, a language spoken primarily in the eastern part of South Yemen a computer was called in to help.

Since misunderstandings had also occurred whenever the ambassadors from Oman and Saudi Arabia spoke Mahri and the ambassador from South Yemen spoke Arabic or whenever the ambassador from Oman and South Yemen spoke Arabic and the ambassador from Saudi Arabia spoke Mahri the computer made the following suggestion. The ambassador from Saudi Arabia should speak Arabic or the ambassador from Oman should speak Arabic and the ambassador from South Yemen should speak Mahri to resolve the problem.

• • •

OKAY!

Co-Host Karen Carns was a statuesque blonde who attracted a lot of attention.

March 15, 1981:

I think that a.m. good morning with Karen Carns is a superior show. Karen is a real good report. She has style, and showmanship; with a good personality, and looks, and charm. She makes the show very interest.

I look at the program every morning before I go to work. There are a lot of people around here that looks at your show.

Thank you very much for bring such a good show; and keep the good work going.P.S. Excuse my writing my typewriter is out of order."

(The letter was written as printed here in longhand.)

Letters could be harsh and crudely personal about a host's appearance.

When are you going to get rid of that Big Swede athletic, no a lady!

She looks like a Swede we get tired of her nakedness. There is not a lady like about her.

Can't you do better. Some thing wrong with all of them.

From time to time in casual "breakfast table"-type conversation the co-hosts engaged in political discussions, particularly during the Watergate hearings. Occasionally these exchanges singed a nerve, but the following letter expresses pathos, even desperation. It begins as an attack on (our) politics, then lashes into a social indictment before moderating into a mother's prayer. I can assure you nothing intentionally vitriolic forced this emotional outburst.

Why do you hate president Nixon so much? It comes over loud and clear. Why did you pick 6 or 7 blacks last night to see what they would say? I'm sure you knew they would be against him. Most blacks in Greensboro are democrats. Will you feel better as you slant the news to hurt the president. I know you are all democrats maybe you can't help it.

You see everything that is wrong and say nothing about what he does good until after you have blasted him for several minutes and stirred up resentment and then you might mention something in passing. You never fail to get all the democrats point across. We republicans have feelings too. We watch the program and news all we ever hear is abuse.

The Greensboro daily (News and Record) expect to get our money and all we hear is abuse and being throwed off on. for over a year nearly two.

I wish we could get a newspaper that is Republican. I have heard that it may come about only then will there be better reporting.

If you are so concerned about Nixon conduct. Why do you put on those filthy soap operas? and other programs. You show everything that leads up to the sex act and then they go under the cover while you put on a commercial.

The stories are a breakdown of morale and our homes. I think it is a slap at marriage and what the Bible has to say about a Christian home being established. That is the only thing that is holding this country together. In spite of what John Edwards {Clinical Psy-

chologist] says that for some to live together before marriage is alright. I don't believe it. God made the vows of love and marriage not John Edwards.

TV is at its lowest ebb since I have had one. It is putting on prime time movies that is not fit for a dog to see. I don't watch but you get enough to know what's going on. Our pastor said Sunday in the sight of God little sins are the same as big one. He said it is all sin in God's sight and he doesn't make a difference. He said that was proven when the woman at the well was not stoned. all had sin in their lives and couldn't accuse here.

But the president has been stoned. I wonder what God really thinks when he looks down on us.

May we humble ourselves and ask God to forgive our self righteousness and bias ways.

A mother heartbroken.

As the "Good Morning Show" evolved into what management referred to as "the station's image," people often sent the show their "letters to the editor." A huge story like the Space program landing a man on the moon was not immune to viewer dissatisfaction.

Winston Salem, July 19, 1966:
We have seen so many of these rockets fly off on your excellently and minutely detailed coverages, sub-coverages, and editorialized repeats reviews and every blasted thing connected with the blast-offs that we frankly cannot hardly abide much more of this fare. I have asked many people if they watch these TV take-offs on the rockets and only about 3% watch at all and then only because they are showing the same darn thing on the other channels anyway. After so many of them they all look alike anyway so please leave some of that stuff off and put on the programs. Ask the public what they want to see. These rocket shots are as flat as left-over beer.
P.S. We are buying the soap chips, dog food, deodorant and stuff they advertise on TV regularly, but a few more moon shots and we are throwing the TV out.

When the launches interfered with the CBS afternoon soap-opera lineup irate viewers choked our switchboard with complaints and the mail poured in. After Neil Armstrong's dramatic walk on the moon one female viewer called in to complain about CBS's extensive coverage. When our operator suggested that a walk on the moon was an historic occasion the viewer replied, "Well, there's a helluva lot more going on 'As The World Turns' than there is on the moon!"

Some letters contained what we interpreted as fragments of thought dredged from the abyss between imagination and reality:

February 21, 1980:
Lee,
Heres a nice poem for you
          The Devil the Black Bird
                    and the Crow
     The snake is a white devil, as we all know,
     I'm the blackbird and you are the crow,
     Maybe you can read the blackbirds mind,
     But God gave the blackbird something that

You will never know.
Yours truly
A Electromagnetic Victim

When the "Good Morning Show" signed on in the late '50s standard English was the accepted language. Our viewers demanded proper respect for sentence structure, agreement, and pronunciation. We spoke more formally than we do now and if we made a grammatical error, or mispronounced a word, viewers called and wrote. I quickly learned that no matter how well you attempt to handle the language correctly you can fall victim to bad habits as a listener and repeat them as a speaker. Living in the nuclear age caused me a lot of grief:

Raleigh, March 1, 1982:
The correct pronunciation of nuclear is noo'kle-ar or nyoo'kle-ar. It is not noo-cu-ler as you and Ms. Carns persist in saying. It is a two-syllable word, not three. Also please check your dictionary and note that the accent on the word "weekend" falls on the first syllable as in wek'end, not on the second syllable. Nor is their emphasis on the final syllable d. (you say weekenduh.)
If you must speak on the air, please do so correctly.

High Point, 17 September 1971:
It has distressed me that for sometime that you do not know how to pronounce nuclear.
"You say nukyoular, when it is new-clee-ar. I tell my chemistry students to say nuclear, properly, and they say, but Lee Kinard says (nukyoular) and then I have to show them the dictionary to prove you are wrong and I am right.
Now you have Karen and the others saying it too. Why not use proper pronunciation?

Until that moment I don't recall ever paying attention to the (correct) pronunciation of nuclear, a word that had been in my vocabulary since 1945. Jargonistically, listening to phrases like "nuke 'em" are probably responsible for transforming my pronunciation of nuclear. Our discussion of the correct pronunciation of "nuclear" elicited several responses.

•   •   •

Raleigh, September 2, 1981:

After today's discussion of differences in pronouncing words, I just want to say that anyone can mispronounce a word but few people have the openness, warmth and sincerity that you three have (Karen Carns, John Nesbit, Lee Kinard). That doesn't mean that you ignore the standard (it is evident that you strive for improvement), but pronunciation shouldn't be the only consideration. I would miss you if you were not there at 6 a.m.

"Good Morning Show" hosts discovered that any "on air" discussion of negative viewer responses would generate a flurry of positive reactions:

I am awarding this blue ribbon to you because you seem to be the only person appearing on TV who pronouncas (or should I say "pronounces") the prefix pro as pro, and the prefix pre as pre.

I can't understand the current trend that eliminates pros and pres from the spoken language, and substitutes per. Products and people pervide, permote, perfect, perduce, perdict, perfer and perpare etc.

I watch many hours of TV daily, and this matter has become my #1 pet peeve. Consequently, each time I hear you utter a loud and clear PRO, I rise to give you a standing ovation.

Wear your Blue Ribbon in good health.

Any perception of pretentiousness determined by members of the TV audience often triggered deflation missiles. The unsigned projectile below was addressed to the general manager. Had it been signed I could have written back that I was just playing around with vocabulary on a day when the weather was totally boring as it is ninety-five percent of the time.

May 23, 1975:

Ambiguous Mother Nature? Who ever heard of that? But that's been the type of poetic vocabulary Lee Kinard has recently began to use in his presentation of the weather. I realize, from experience, that attending college has an affect on a person, but does it have to result in poetizing the weather? I've grown up with Lee Kinard on the screen and it all sounds so foreign, for example: '...the romance of the heightened morning....flee to the coast to escape it...the day is being marred...or beginning my morning with the odor of honeysuckle...' To the majority of the television viewers, probably who have never entered college, more than likely those 'big words' do not register.

So what have we got here? Perhaps another Ted Knight? One is enough. Well, maybe 'progress' is to blame for this change. It sure will take a while to get accustomed to or maybe just a switch of the channel would suit my fancy.

Anyway, see ya at UNC-G next fall, Lee Kinard.

A disturbed viewer.

Through no fault of my own I have inspired dozens of poems and songs during the last 40 years. This tome appeared in a regional tabloid.

Ode to Lee Kinard
I love Lee in the morning
I love Lee nights at six
It's Lee again at seven
That's how I get my kicks.

His Eye is on the Piedmont
His buzz-cut's straight and trim
He's been around since Adam
I wish that I were him
He used to do the weather
Now he does the news
It really doesn't matter
Channel 2 can choose
You can take Rick Amme
And torture him insane
Bind and gag Fred Blackman
And leave him lying lame.
Eliminate Ms. Franklin
Denise, farewell to thee
Come on now, altogether
It's Lee, It's Lee, It's Lee.

This next composition was written to commemorate the 20th anniversary of the "Good Morning Show."

Greensboro, December 9, 1977
An anniversary is looming, they tell me
An important date in television history.
Twenty years on camera is quite a feat.
And for Greensboro it has been a treat.

To stagger to the kitchen with half-open eyes,
To down some O.J. amid yawns and sighs,
To struggle with packing up lunch boxes
While checking children for measles and poxes.
Pattering around with the dog underfoot
And a husband who announces that he is Kaput—
These make one wish to retire from the scene—
But wait—there's Lee Kinard on the screen!
And somehow, his presence and eternal good cheer
Come bursting into the room loud and clear;
The staggering ceases and the whining stops
Because everyone knows that Lee is tops.
His interesting guests refresh our minds,
Day after day, Lee presents all kinds
Of folks who make our community go,
And it's really been great to know
That he is always there, early each day
To chase the morning fog away.
Best Wishes on this landmark of twenty—
Please keep on for years a plenty,
'Cause I don't think Greensboro could get up and go
Without Lee Kinard and the Good Morning Show.

Lee Kinard
By Joseph Fryar
"He's greater than Cronkite
And Sevareid too
Dan Rather could learn things from him
He's smoother than Como
Has Fred Astair's move
He'll dance at the tiniest whim.
The folks in the Triad
All heed his voice
He wakes them up with the news
If you do something dirty
And cover your trail
And you're certain that nobody knows
You may be surprised
To see every detail

*Next day on the Good Morning
Show*
He'll tell how you did it
Where, when and why
Your secrets all come out
He knows where you visit
If you sail or fly
All you can do then is pout
He does it finer
Than all Carolina
News, weather and sports on TV
Nothing in Carolina
Rhymes with the name Kinard
So let's just call him Lee
A champion of champions
A king among Dukes
He's number one with the news
The great commentator
On missiles and nukes
But I wouldn't be in his shoes
He rises so early
With heavy eyelids
He mechanically pulls on his socks
His first task is magic
I do not kid
He wakes up all the alarm clocks
Leaves home before daylight
Beneath starlit skies
He activates morning dew
When the rest of the Piedmont

Open their eyes
He's already on Channel Two
And so now Lee Kinard
My hat's off to you
The world will bow at your feet
A request for tomorrow
When you're compiling the news
Remember that I'm still asleep
Birds of a feather
Do flock together
So I've heard people tell
If you are a joiner
Enlister, belonger
Be careful about PTL

I am obviously overwhelmed with comparisons to Sevareid and Cronkite. Cronkite and I were once neighbors at the same motel in Cocoa Beach, Florida, during the Great American Race to Space in the 1960s, but I could never manage to latch onto him for an interview.

One lesson I have learned from a lifetime of performing is that a smile can go a long way toward making friends.

Does He Always Smile?
When you have a real bad day

And you are feeling low and blue
Just turn your dial to Channel 2
Lee has a smile for you.
When its good or when its bad
I have never seen another
Who is always smiling
When he talks about the weather.
Of course he isn't always right
But he don't seem to mind
If he tells you it will rain
And the sun comes out and shines.
When I look at him so happy
I'll always wonder too
Does he have that smile at home
When his days work is through.
You may not tell the weather
When you reach your home above
But with that happy face on earth
You've won the people's love.
You may never win a medal
Or be in the hall of fame
But you just keep right on smiling
We don't want you to ever change.

Well, that's all folks. Keep those cards and letters and that E-mail coming, but just be sure you sign your name.

TWELVE

Memorable Moments

Lee reviewing "Good Morning Show" program with Director Billy Overman.

I can't imagine enjoying a more rewarding experience than hosting and producing the "Good Morning Show" for 40 years. And don't think for an instant that those decades have melted into a congealed mass. The "Good Morning Show" is linearly patched to historic time lines beginning with the dawning of the American Space Age in 1957. Having filed the show's paperwork, notes, memos, detailed minutes of meetings, and letters, and having been there I have a pretty good grasp of this phenomenal passage.

Its memorable moments are frankly rather mellow. After all this has never been a contentious program though it represents a lot of hard, hard work. One of the show's most awkward moments occurred during a live broadcast of the Holiday Market at the Greensboro Coliseum Special Events Center. WFMY-TV often co-sponsors this major attraction where hundreds of commercial vendors set up stalls to market holiday merchandise. It was the perfect venue to stage a "Good Morning Show" Fan Appreciation Day and invite an audience to enjoy a special edition of the show. We took our entire hosting contingent to the coliseum for the event, but since risk is part of every remote telecast we planned for contingencies.

We scheduled a producer and news reader to standby at the studios and prepared a backup format with features that could be inserted if we lost our live signal. A great audience showed up, dyed in the wool fans were in their seats at 5:30 a.m. and we were rising sky high! That is until the fudge vendor powered up his oven and blew away the electrical system. The power failure knocked us into "black" in front of a live audience who thought it was great fun seeing us wimpy and scrambling.

Apologetically, we have promoted some bizarre attractions to hook audiences during sweeps periods, but if I had it to do all over again I don't think I would talk two members of our production crew into getting married on the show. Let's just say that Robert Reed and Teresa Jessup volunteered to say their nuptials before live cameras as the final segment in a five-part series called "June Brides." The ceremony was televised from the patio of the Bryan Enrichment Center in Greensboro at 7:30 on a cloudy Friday morning in the merry month of May.

One lighter, brighter, carefree morning 40 years ago almost cost me my job. I was reminded of the incident by Jim Edmunds, one of the "Good Morning Show's" former directors. It involved my good buddy Bob Waddell, one of the talented creative geniuses of early WFMY-TV days.

My first remembrance of the show is as a member of the floor crew. There was "Greenie" Bob Waddell and his antics as a camera operator. Like the mornings he would take the camera to the far end of the studio and put it behind the drapes and shoot the show with only the lens showing. Then there were the mornings when he would un-

zip his fly and pull his pocket through trying to break you up while you were doing the news and weather.

When Waddell pulled this stunt, I broke into hysterical, uncontrollable laughter. Watching at home General Manager Gaines Kelley was infuriated. On his way to the station he reportedly hailed his operations manager at a stoplight and told him he was going to fire me as soon as he got to the station. In no uncertain terms Kelley demanded an explanation for the outburst. I was literally scared to death. I told as straightforward a lie as I could muster, something to the effect that, "It takes a certain kind of personality to work in the morning and I was so charged up with glibness and giddiness that it didn't take much to break me up."

Kelley knew Waddell was the prankster and gave me every opportunity to implicate him, but I refused to rat on the nut. Believe me, I didn't defend him out of any great sense of love, but I figured sooner or later I'd get him back. I left the front office after a royal reaming but I left with my job. For weeks the "Good Morning Show" was under surveillance by the operations manager who hid out in the viewing gallery high above the studio hoping to catch Waddell in one of his shenanigans. You have to remember we were still in our 20s and having fun at every opportunity.

In the '80s one of my gags got me tagged as "The Dancing Weatherman." Writer Sherry Roberts picked up on the act and described it in a magazine article. It was just another spontaneous gag that became a regular "bit." Prior to my weather presentation we played various pop tunes behind a series of weather statistics. One day the "Good Morning Show's" longtime audio engineer, Jack Dixon cued up some beach music. When the camera took me I was shagging to the beat.

The bit caught on with the crew and some of the viewers. One "Good Morning Show" fan who literally hated my moves wrote that her entire factory shift had decided to stop watching the "Good Morning Show" because of my dancing. I had to give up the gag when I was stricken with a painful series of migraine headaches that made it difficult to stand up and talk much less dance.

Sometimes it takes a tragedy to discover how meritorious people really are. After vandals defaced the statue of General Nathaniel Greene at the Guilford Battleground National Park in Greensboro former Mayor Jim Melvin suggested the "Good Morning Show" stage a campaign to raise funds to restore the memorial.

One dewy August morning following the vandalism we staged a live telethon from the memorial to plead for cash. Our production included a Dixieland band, a barbershop quartet and other entertainers who donated their time. We set up a phone bank to take donations from viewers and raised around $15,000. It was an inspiring morning proving that television is at its best when it is working in the spirit of community and making fraternity happen.

Some of the "Good Morning Show's" most memorable moments have been its anniversary shows. The 20th anniversary celebration (1977) was probably the biggest surprise. The personal accolades the community showered on me surpassed any recognition I ever hoped to achieve in my life. Publishing "The Good Morning Show Cookbook and Anecdotal History" in 1987 and 1992 is noteworthy because it enabled us to show our appreciation to our fans. And, oh yes, the recipes were pretty doggone good!

Earlier I reminisced about walking to work in the snow and the snowball fights we staged before the "Good Morning Show" got serious about the weather. Some of the more memorable mornings were the days I sat on a stool outside the studio door sipping coffee, reading school closings and watching the traffic slide around the corner of Phillips Avenue and White Street.

The new studio set General Manager Colleen Brown endorsed and Deborah Hooper remodeled ranks high as memorable also. Guests are amazed when they see how the show operates from its beautiful and functional 60-by-40-foot home. The set includes a stylish living room, a serviceable kitchen, a library area, and a gallery. A news and weather set are the show's more utilitarian fixtures. The sets are built around the studio in a fashion that allows us to walk quickly from one area to the next.

Many memorable moments are built around the ratings, or sweeps. TV viewership in the Piedmont is measured every quarter by the Neilsen Company. Diaries are sent to selected households in our coverage area across a four-week period in February, May, July and September. Participants record their demographic data and list the shows they watch for a week. The diaries are returned for auditing and a massive amount of statistical marketing information is compiled from the survey.

The ratings are the show's report cards. Getting a report card in school is hazardous: getting 160 of them in 40 years on the "Good Morning Show" is the mother lode of anxiety. I don't like the system, but it's the only one available and I have to live with it. Surviving ratings was easier when the "Good Morning Show" was the only early morning local TV show in the Piedmont and cable penetration was insignificant. That is not the case now and viewers have dozens of choices.

Ratings are divided into percentages and shares. For example the "Good Morning Show's" first rating in spring 1958 four months after the show premiered was a 2; that meant two percent of the total sets in our designated coverage area tuned in the "Good Morning Show." We worked to pull that figure higher and succeeded thanks to the "Mystery Personality Contest." In 1959 we were viewed by eight percent of the possible audience, a respectable figure for early morning local TV shows.

When our snow storm coverage captured the attention of the Piedmont in 1960 and local TV news became credible our ratings sky rocketed. In the mid-to-late '80s a 12 or 13 rating with a 55-60 percent audience share set a phenomenal record. In the '90s our ratings are back to single digits with audience shares around 40 percent. Considering the quality and quantity of competition that's a hefty endorsement. The "Good Morning Show" still maintains its first place ranking, but there's always another wrinkle. Now marketing experts look closely at our demographics to sell commercials.

Well folks, the cameraman is signalling a wrap-up, a circular motion with the index finger, and that means it's time to go, but first a few thoughts about where we stand as 1997 winds to a close.

In its 40th year the "Good Morning Show" is broadcasting daily from 5:30 to 8 am. More than half of that time is devoted to weather, news, sports, traffic reports and other information pertinent to escorting viewers into the working day. Four hosts anchor the show from all angles of a massive set, interviewing, demonstrating, entertaining, and presenting encyclopedic chunks of information. There is cooking and gardening, psychotherapy, self-help and community notes. There is credibility and warmth and affection from hosts who truly revere and support their viewing family.

On a personal level, what can I say? I got paid for every day, but it's been more than a job. It's been a lifetime love. It fed, clothed and housed my family and put my children through college. It educated me, taught me about myself, helped me learn to love you. It sent me around the world more than a few times and brought me home safely. It helped some of you learn how to read the Bible, prevented you from wrecking on the ice and convinced you to finish school. It may have helped you find that lump in your breast before it was too late, or scared you into a prostate checkup. Ouch!

The food has been too rich to lower your cholesterol, but our intentions were good, according to Chefs John Drees, Mary James Lawrence, Babs Wilkinson, Emmie Whitley and Nancy King Quaintance. From time to time when the world sent our heads spinning John Edwards and Bob Quindlen were always on call for introspection. When downsizing set you on the bench we rang up Joyce Richman to find you a job. Ted Graham, William Mangum, Bob TimberLake, and Jill Troutman have brightened your walls and our poets and authors have filled your shelves.

We've played you some sad songs and sung all the good songs and somewhere our troubadours Bob Waddell and Bill Kirkpatrick are dueting the Anniversary Song. Now, it's time to get back to the office and plan the next shows. We'll open with brainstorming and make a list of the challenges that face our Piedmont communities. And when we've decided how we can help you, we'll conjure up some features to snag you for three and a half minutes. Then, we'll open the voice mail and the old-fashioned letter mail, note your suggestions and mail out the recipes. Producer Jack Hilliard will force us to tell him what we're really doing on tomorrow's show and we'll leave us some holes to have more fun. Then, we'll hang it up and head for the barn and, when passing by the receptionist's desk, give Barbara Fuller a hug for telling everyone who calls she'll make us behave.

That's the "Good Morning Show" for today. Thanks for tuning in and "Have the greatest day of your life!"

Okay Dixon, it's time to turn the mike off and pop that champagne cork!

EPILOGUE

From the bottom of my heart I would like to thank the generations of viewers who have made the "Good Morning Show" an exceptional ride. Thanks for making me and my family a part of your family.

Thanks to Gaines Kelley and Gomer Lesch for making the "Good Morning Show" happen; to WFMY-TV's "mother superior" Jeta Pace for challenging me to produce decent and hopefully inspiring television; to Jay Wilkinson, Jack Forehand, Frank Bennett, Jack Hilliard and Mike Conly for friendship and confidence, to Jewel Kirk and Armand Bodie for keeping WFMY-TV solvent; to Shirley Frye and Dona Pickett for shoulders to lean on; to Gannett and Cecil Walker for your bountiful support and for Presidents/ General Managers Hank Price, Colleen Brown and Deborah Hooper.

At this point in my life and career I can't imagine that I would have been happier or more fulfilled had I done anything else. When I leave WFMY-TV it will be with a sense of pride for what our program has been able to present as a gift to the community in terms of service, information, ideas and money. From what viewers tell me the "Good Morning Show" has changed innumerable lives and inspired thousands to seek new directions.

I suppose that some day I won't be getting up five days a week to do the "Good Morning Show." I'll probably wander around in a daze for a few weeks, wondering, how did I do that gig for 40 years of weekday mornings, or was it only a dream?

Greensboro, Sunday, July 6, 1997